Developing Your Design Process

Developing Your Design Process is your primary source for acquiring knowledge of how and why you design. It will help you understand how architects think as well as learn why you should educate yourself about design culture. You'll explore the spark of imagination that leads to a strong concept, realize the importance of sketching and rough drafts, focus your original concept to make your abstract idea visible, and finally step away for a moment to critically question your concept by identifying its strengths and weaknesses. You'll also be introduced to the language of design, architectural terminology, historic precedents, and designers, in addition to the why, what, and how of the design process.

The book is illustrated throughout with international examples of work by professionals and students in the discipline of architecture, and other related design professions.

Albert C. Smith is an Associate Professor in the Department of Architectural Science at Ryerson University, Canada. He holds a PhD, from the Georgia Institute of Technology, in architecture with a subject area of history, theory and criticism, he has a main interest in representation and is author of the book *Architectural Model as Machine*.

Kendra Schank Smith is an Associate Professor in the Department of Architectural Science at Ryerson University. With a PhD in architecture from Georgia Tech, she has written on representation, urbanism, architectural education, and media, and has published two books that explore the representational qualities of architectural sketches.

Developing Your Design Process

Six key concepts for studio

Albert C. Smith and Kendra Schank Smith

Routledge
Taylor & Francis Group

NEW YORK AND LONDON

First published 2015

by Routledge
711 Third Avenue, New York, NY 10017

and by Routledge
2 Park Square, Milton Park, Abingdon, Oxon OX14 4RN

Routledge is an imprint of the Taylor & Francis Group, an informa business

Library of Congress Cataloging in Publication Data
Smith, Albert C.
Developing your design process : six key concepts for studio / Albert C.
Smith and Kendra Schank Smith.
pages cm
Includes bibliographical references and index.
1. Architectural design. I. Smith, Kendra Schank. II. Title.
NA2750.S575 2014
729--dc23
2013038038

ISBN: 978-0-415-84071-2 (hbk)
ISBN: 978-0-415-84072-9 (pbk)
ISBN: 978-1-315-79665-9 (ebk)

Acquisition Editor: Wendy Fuller
Editorial Assistant: Grace Harrison
Production Editor: Alanna Donaldson

Typeset in Calvert
by Oliver Hutton

MIX
Paper from
responsible sources
FSC
www.fsc.org   FSC® C013056

Printed and bound in Great Britain by
TJ International Ltd, Padstow, Cornwall

Acknowledgments

We would like to thank Jessica Stanford and Mitchell May for their thoughts during early discussions about design process. We want to express special appreciation to Gerald Karaguni for his assistance with digital reproduction, photography, and editing. Our sincere appreciation goes to Hilary Neal, who has drafted passages, edited, and provided helpful insight since the beginning of the project. We would also like to thank Ryerson University for assistance with research funding and an Undergraduate Research Opportunities program grant.

We would like to dedicate this book to our parents and Marco Frascari.

Contents

List of Illustrations

Opening

Creativity is a habit.
It's not something that
happens in the shower.

Nick Law

Whether you are a beginning design student or an established professional, understanding the design process can be challenging. Questions about this fascinating process arise as to how designers generate ideas, what techniques they use to develop concepts into usable products and structures, and why design matters to society. Creativity can appear mysterious to the uninitiated, and is not easily explained or taught. To successfully learn about design typically requires years of dedication and it is primarily through experiential learning. It is much like learning to ride a bicycle. You can learn all there is to know about the mechanics of a bicycle, the physics of balance involved, and step-by-step

instructions of what to do, but the only way to actually learn is by getting on the bike and trying.

0.1 Students from the Department of Architectural Science, Ryerson University

The purpose of *Developing Your Design Process: Six Key Concepts for Studio* is to explore aspects of the design process and provide thoughts about design culture and the act of making. The topics do not necessarily present a linear description of a method of design, but instead touch on ways to find ideas, techniques for utilizing design media, defining and editing solutions, and evaluating projects along the way. The intention of this book is to help make the experience of the design studio more easily understood for beginners.

Those who would find this book most useful are architectural educators, practitioners, students of architecture, and designers, but since it discusses design in the broad sense, it can be relevant to many fields. An understanding of the basic principles of design is the reason why so many architects are easily able to design chairs, interiors, graphics, and industrial designs, as well as buildings. To design means to create, fashion, execute, and construct something that is intentional, functional, and aesthetically pleasing and constitutes a general broad-based way of thinking of which architecture is but a part. In this way, it is important to not think just in terms of formulistic principles but of how to think like a designer.

In recent years, it has been increasingly acknowledged by society that design matters, and business and industry have been recognizing the value of design to global economies.[1] Governments are beginning to realize that quality design improves the lives of their citizens, be it through a better park bench or a safer road system. Business is learning that good design sells, and the public, through awareness and exposure to competition, are demanding better and better quality in all their products, so much so that courses in entrepreneurial studies often include design exercises. Apple's iPod, iPad, and computers have introduced many to high quality and innovative products that are durable and attractive to consumers all over the world.[2] To the average layperson, the creativity that envisions these products must seem to emerge almost like magic, but no great thing is created suddenly.[3] Although it is possible to imagine a designer conjuring something seemingly out of nowhere, the creative process, and indeed the design process, are based in effort and trial and error. When in the midst of determining concepts in the early stages of design, designers rely on the manipulation of media, and it is through this transformation of materials that inspiration emerges. Design also relies on broad knowledge, hard work, and observation of the human environment.

Marcus Vitruvius Pollio, the Roman writer, architect, and engineer, writes in his influential *Ten Books of Architecture* that to understand the design process means that you need a broad-based education, knowledge of many fields, and developed skills combined with natural talent.[4] Acquiring this broad knowledge, and learning the skills of the profession, takes time and dedication. Designers and architects also need to be able to persuade influential people to support good design. The areas of knowledge important for designers and architects include anything that involves the human and built environment, as well as a wide range of subjects. Because architecture and the design fields require tremendous skill and knowledge, and because the creative process seems elusive to the general public, success in this mysterious discipline has historically appeared secretive.

0.2 Baumeister/Architect

During the Gothic, Romanesque, and Renaissance periods in Europe, architects were members of guilds, specifically organized to safeguard the secrets of builders and designers. In addition to these guilds, the Romanesque and Gothic craftsmen collected design details as templates in sketchbooks as they moved from city to city.[5] Those with the talent and knowledge to produce great designs seemed to possess divine powers.[6] We can look to today's starchitects such as Frank Gehry or Zaha Hadid to offer good examples of this. A contemporary phenomenon, the *starchitect* is a successful practitioner who has reached celebrity status. This ultra-famous professional is world-renowned through a recognizable style and has the status to influence the economies of cities and regions with their designs. These architects have successfully brought the discipline of design and architecture to a wide public audience, but the secrets of their process remain elusive. The public has little knowledge of the process required to develop a design from initial sketches on paper napkins to the resulting complex building.

Design is important to everything we do, buy, and encounter, and is evident on all scales from a paperclip to city and regional planning. If we look to one of the most common and simple office tools, the Gem Paperclip, it is possible to view some important aspects of design as a critical thinking process. Various forms of paperclips have been refined since the late 1800s but in its many versions, the Gem Paperclip's function and effectiveness have not been significantly improved upon. The success of its design emerges from being functional, structurally sound, inexpensive to produce, durable, aesthetically pleasing in its proportions and curves, safe to use, and brilliant in its minimal efficiency. Architectural design can be similarly viewed as not necessarily aesthetics alone, but successful when everything works together in a surprising and striking way – an act of great balance. Comparably, a definition of design from Leon Battista Alberti states that a design is successful and complete when nothing can be added or taken away.[7] The design process epitomizes critical thinking and involves the "intellectually disciplined process of actively and skillfully conceptualizing, applying, analyzing, synthesizing, and/or evaluating information gathered from, or generated

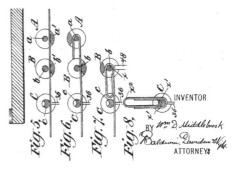

0.3 1899 US patent for paper clip machine

by, observation, experience, reflection, reasoning or communication, as a guide to belief and action."[8] This may sound like a complex and involved process – and it is – but it describes the way designers and architects engage their approach to design.

Design concerns imagining the future and visualizing things that have not been seen before. It is a non-linear process, as it tends to move forward and backward between topics. Once again, it is unique in that the process includes different forms of knowledge and experience from imagining conceptual ideas to evaluation and refinement throughout the process. The designer Chuck Green writes that "good design is partially creativity and innovation, but primarily knowledge and awareness."[9] It has been mentioned that design also requires talent because while design techniques can be learned, certain people have a propensity for this type of thinking. Some may suggest that it is entirely intuitive, but most would agree that design requires innate talent combined with hard work and the utilization of knowledge and experience. Solutions to the design of a specific building cannot be taken directly from a book – they are not based in recitation nor can they be copied in their entirety. Finding successful solutions requires discipline, conscious effort, analytical skills, and talent. Mastering the ability to arrive at a "good design" is elusive[10] and could be compared to the creative process in literature described by Roderich Fuess, where he compares a quick sketch to the uncertainty of design: "For [James] Joyce the first sketch is not the initiation into the process of writing, it is much more comparable to pinning down an almost invisible butterfly with an unsteady stylus."[11]

WHY DESIGN?

The stereotype of architectural education is that of students spending hours at the drawing board making floor plans and many enter into architectural or design programs having taken classes in drafting or computer software. It is no surprise then, that students are often confused when their first assignment in an introductory studio course looks something like this:

> Imagine a salt flats gleaming white in the sun. It never rains in this perfectly flat place that stretches for hundreds of miles in all directions. It is the Tabula Rasa, the blank slate. In the middle of this place are dug two perfectly square pits, each representing the opposite of the other as up/down, black/white, good/evil, etc. Through an unexcavated space between them you will design an entry for humans to travel from one space to the other. Each entry should represent the idea of the other place.[12]

Instead of technical requirements, beginning design students may be faced with ambiguous descriptions of spaces or conditions that require their intervention. There are often no set steps to guide the process, and no correct answer. Instead, this type of assignment forces students to think about the *why* of the environments they are making, in addition to *how* these experiences will be produced. Instructors assign problems like this to get students to think critically about how their spaces feel and how they can convey a concept through the design of an appropriate intervention. The ambiguity of an assignment like this enables students to start to develop their own design process by coming up with their own ideas and concepts. This type of project also breaks down preconceived notions that students have acquired from their former experiences. The problem for many beginning students is that they are unaware of the uncertainties and potentialities of design.

Developing Your Design Process: Six Key Concepts for Studio can thus be thought of as a primer for students entering the design field or as a reminder for professionals about how to think about their own design processes. Design is a multifaceted process that can remain elusive even after years of practice and while there are no specified methods

0.4 Students from the Department of Architectural Science, Ryerson University

that guarantee a successful outcome, there are ways of thinking critically throughout the process that when used appropriately, can result in more thoughtful projects. This book aims to give students clear and direct ways to negotiate thinking about design and what to expect from the design studio experience.

Again, because of its non-linear process, design can be considered ambiguous. Assignments will be ambiguous. Advice will be ambiguous. Professors will be ambiguous. While a designer can use ambiguity to help with the development of conceptual ideas, design also implies a certain precision, so that it is not removed from the realities of life. In other words, it is your responsibility to engage this ambiguity and make the project clear. It is important for people interested in design to understand the complexities of this process since it reflects a unique blend of research, analysis, synthesis, and innovation.

Part of the act of clarifying is accomplished through designing the way something should look, function, and be constructed. The act of designing usually means establishing boundaries, parameters, or rules to explain what the project will be. A story in the book *Architectural Model as Machine* speculates about a discovery by an early person that may help to illustrate the importance of boundaries.

Long ago, before anyone built their first dwelling, there lived a very intelligent human. One day the human was walking in the woods and found a marvelous stick. The stick was long – about as long as the human was tall. It was straight, strong, and pointed at one end. There was something about this particular stick that made the human want to pick it up and keep it. Rather quickly the human found that the stick could be used as a staff to facilitate walking. It was also useful in digging for delicious roots and helpful in knocking down berries from high branches. Once the human, when attacked by a vicious animal, found that the stick could be used for defense. The human realized the stick made a wonderful and controllable extension of the hand. The stick was a tool, and a most prized possession. Still wandering, the human arrived in a large pleasant clearing and decided to rest. Not finding a tree close by against which to lean the stick, the human decided to drive it directly into the ground. All day long the human rested and watched the shadow of the stick change. The once controllable stick was beginning to raise wondrous, but not necessarily easily understandable, questions about the universe. The stick took on a life of its own; it presented a better way of understanding the sun, creating questions about a vast chaotic universe. It changed from a tool into a scaling machine and seemed to encourage the possibility of understanding the measure of things. From then on, whenever the human met other humans, the stick would be ceremoniously thrust into the ground. They, then, were also compelled to think about their relationship to their universe and to make a variety of attempts at further explanation.[13]

The stick represents a mechanism that assists us to understand many of the things in our world that are not easily understood. It offered this early person the ability to begin formulating an understandable measurement for defining the invisible and unknown. In a similar way, the mechanisms we use to design such as models and drawings – and in fact, the buildings that we live in – help us to comprehend more about our culture, society, and the ways in which we live. The unknowns of future buildings must be defined. Thus, boundaries that help us design are like the rules we work within and will be a reoccurring theme throughout the entire book.

By understanding the methods and tools used by others, this book aims to empower you to embrace the unknown, to use ambiguity to challenge what is existing, and most importantly, to allow you to develop your own method for designing. By fostering an understanding of the design process for those interested in design, be it a student, or a client, the aim is to understand why we do what we do, and how we do it.

THE ORDER OF THINGS

There has been a long and illustrious tradition of explaining the importance of design to the unversed. One can think of the great writings of historical figures such as architects Vitruvius and Leon Battista Alberti who attempted to present the importance of the design process to the Emperor of

Rome or the Popes of the Renaissance. This book is not attempting to equal these great texts, but rather present ideas about what goes on in the design process in an accessible way to the beginning design student, professional, design client, or anyone else interested in the creative process.

To understand how the book is organized one should think of a necklace. Think of the chapters and subheadings as separate beads that can be successfully engaged individually. The connecting string, tying the beads together, may be seen as representing the overall importance of the design process, bringing the individual parts together into a cohesive whole. The book is divided into six chapters with each chapter containing a series of thoughts important to understanding the main themes.

The first chapter is entitled, "Beginning." It is intended to offer the reader general thoughts about how and why design is important. The chapter explores the relevance of being educated in the culture of design and discusses how designers develop goals and ideals pertaining to their work. This process involves the ability to educate oneself to look, see, and experience things in the world in order to create better designs. The chapter talks about how students and laypeople might go about learning the verbal and visual language used to communicate design and offers the reader suggestions about how to engage in design thinking. This is particularly important because design thinking is not based in rote learning, but encourages broad consideration of possibilities and a holistic vision of function, efficiency, and aesthetics. Finally, this section explores why designers need to develop a position based on their beliefs about their work.

Chapter two, "Imagining," concerns the development of a clear design concept. It is an exploration of the *eureka moment* stimulating the imagination that may eventually lead to thoughtful concepts. The chapter talks about historical references such as why and how the ancient Greeks called upon their muses. The chapter will discuss the importance of what can be learned by looking back at the successes and failures of past designs. All design is forward thinking, embracing change and imagining the future, and this chapter discusses why designers must also look forward to better understand their proposed designs. The chapter emphasizes the dialogue and discourse that designers maintain with their concepts to produce successful designs and ultimately concludes with suggestions about how to "light the spark": methods for creating clear and useful design concepts.

The third chapter is entitled "Playing" and investigates the concept of sketching and rough drafts. This section begins with the general idea of what it means to sketch and the creation of rough drafts as a method to explore early ideas. It discusses how sketching a variety of possible concepts is similar to creating a series of rough drafts of a written work. The chapter argues that the act of design, in many ways, represents a serious form of play. A key aspect of understanding sketches, whether physical, computer models, or those completed by hand, is their ability to allow quick views of multiple possibilities.

Chapter four is entitled "Choosing" and touches on the fine-tuning of design concepts. The chapter includes information about the importance of creating initial boundaries around your specific design concept. It presents ways to successfully analyze the strengths and weaknesses of projects, including filtering through various design concepts. Subsequently, after discussing the successful filtering of ideas, it focuses on methods to improve the best initiatives. Finally, it investigates how much of design is making educated guesses to eliminate specific choices in favor of other ones.

The fifth chapter, "Defining," explores how and why architects delineate their proposed design. It describes the importance of the connections between design intentions and the final product. It discusses ways to develop a clear definition of the intended intervention. The chapter talks about smoothing and polishing to reinforce the process of defining as it is related to making the invisible possibilities of design visible. This section concludes with suggestions on ways to clearly describe design intention.

The final chapter, "Assessing," provides suggestions to help critically analyze the faults inherent in concepts and designs. To successfully assess, designers should not become too infatuated with their creations, but instead step back and consider the design with a critical eye. As a designer, it is important to be able identify the strengths and weaknesses of a specific design project by questioning proposed concepts. The chapter offers strategies for reassessing the products of design in order to improve them and talks about making good decisions throughout the design process.

WHERE TO START?

It should now be clear that an understanding of design is uniquely different than assembly by formula or recipe. Because of this, suggestions for improving design depend upon experimenting and manipulating design media. So the question arises, how do we engage this universally understood yet enigmatic process? The techniques and recommendations in the book should be viewed as a companion to experience and discovery. Each chapter reveals thoughts about theory – exploring the why of the process, in addition to the how. Following a discussion of why, each chapter presents studio examples and architects' experience. The method is to propose topics for discussion, using analogies and metaphors to illustrate possible approaches to design. These techniques will assist you to anticipate how to deal with uncertainty, find ways to challenge yourself, and remind you of ways to think visually. While not intended as a "how-to" book, *Developing Your Design Process: Six Key Concepts for Studio* will explore various aspects of design that provide insight into architecture and design culture, and investigate ways to spark the imagination, techniques for manipulating design media, defining and editing your design solution, and evaluating suitable solutions to your ideas.

Endnotes

1   John Heskett, "Creating Economic Value by Design," *International Journal of Design* 3, no. 1 (2009): 71–84.

2   Laura Sydell. "Steve Jobs' Greatest Legacy May Be Impact on Design," National Public Radio, www.npr.org/2011/10/06/141118621/steve-jobs-greatest-legacy-may-be-impact-on-design.

3   The musician and researcher Charles Limb states that "creativity is magical, but is not magic." Utilizing imagination and inventing new forms requires the ability to recognize and encourage ways to make magical things happen – as it is known that no great thing is created suddenly. While the process of designing and unexpected inspirations may appear like magic, we should never pretend that designs will appear instantaneously; instead design requires effort and hard work. In fact, traditional definitions of magic have been associated with the ability of magic to be productive, the action of "doing," and thus the act of design may seem magical. Marcel Mauss, *A General Theory of Magic* (New York: W.W. Norton, 1972), 18–24.

4   "He should be a man of letters, a skillful draughtsman, a mathematician, familiar with scientific inquiries, a diligent student of philosophy, acquainted with music; not ignorant of medicine, learned in the responses of jurisconsults, familiar with astronomy and astronomical calculations." Marcus Vitruvius Pollio, *On Architecture*, trans. Frank Granger (Cambridge, MA: Harvard University Press, 1931), 7–9.

5   See *The Sketchbook of Villard de Honnecourt*, ed. Theodore Bowle (Bloomington and London: Indiana University Press, 1959).

6   Ernst Kris and Otto Kurz, *Legend, Myth and Magic in the Image of the Artist* (New Haven: Yale University Press, 1979), 61–90.

7   Leon Battista Alberti, *On the Art of Building in Ten Books*, trans. Joseph Rykwert, Neil Leach, and Robert Tavernor (Cambridge, MA: MIT Press, 1991), 156.

8   Michael Scriven and Richard Paul, "Critical Thinking" (presentation at the eighth Annual International Conference on Critical Thinking and Education Reform, Summer 1987).

9   Chuck Green, Twitter post, March 28, 2010, 11:34am, https://twitter.com/ideabook.

10 Chapter two will discuss "good" architecture.

11 Roderich Fuess, "Epiphany: To the First Sketch in Modern Literature," *Daidalos* 5 (1982): 26.

12 First year studio project at Ryerson University written by Albert C. Smith.

13 Albert C. Smith, *Architectural Model as Machine* (Oxford: The Architectural Press Elsevier, 2004), xv–xvi.

Beginning
Chapter 1

In order to succeed,

your desire for success

should be greater than

your fear of failure.

Bill Cosby ← interesting

This first chapter explores what to expect when you begin any design process. In general, before design begins, a need must be identified. This need or desire is a recognized social opportunity, commission, or studio assignment, for example, and can be the impetus to begin a project. As either a student or a design professional the process starts with a *program*, usually a written statement, that presents the parameters of the project and suggests an approach. Some programs can be quite open-ended and others more restrictive, anticipating an intended outcome.

Studio education, the theme of this book, is experiential in nature. Your professors

1.1 Thomas Edison and his early phonograph

will provide assignments for you and your classmates to come up with appropriate solutions, depending upon your interpretation of a given program. To accomplish this, you will need all your creative abilities, which can be acquired as you study design.

To create is "to produce a work of imagination, invention or artifact,"[1] such as works of art, literature, a piece of furniture, or the design of a building. Architecture and design students should not make the mistake of assuming a person is creative simply because they call themselves a designer. Nor is becoming a creative person solely about aspiration; rather it is developing a way to think, which can take a great deal of effort and practice, and of course, talent. Although a popular adage, Thomas Edison has been credited with saying, "Creativity is 99% perspiration and 1% inspiration."[2] The effort is necessary because design does not happen in a void without outside influences.

Design is both a noun, describing an object, and it is also a verb, portraying a process. The goal of design school is not only to develop a successful final product, but also, and perhaps more importantly, to learn a process of design. This involves, first and foremost, determining what one desires to create. In other words, you should have a concept about what you want to achieve. To understand what you desire to do, it is critical to develop ideals, a belief system, or a position about the future of design. These will not be the same for everyone, and to be successful it is critical to educate yourself in order to develop a clear vision about these ideals and values. Will they be useful and what strengths and flaws could they contain? Design schools help students to view the possibilities, learn to think critically, and cultivate a repertoire of experiences. To develop design experiences, you need to learn the language and conventions of the discipline; in other words, you must begin to think like a designer.

ANTICIPATING

Students have been working late in the studio and Sandra has been sitting alone contemplating the guidelines for a model that is due the next day. She is concentrating on how to find a creative solution for the design of a small monument but is becoming frustrated after hours of work. Sandra looks over at her classmates and is surprised to see that Soon is tearing pieces of cardboard, John is leafing through magazines, and Negar, Mohamed, and Joy are playing word games. On the other side of the room Tom is piling stools to an unbelievable height, Mike keeps turning his model upside down and Madison is intently watching the way leaves flutter in the trees. Sandra wonders how they can waste so much time when she wants to find an idea as quickly as possible and get home to sleep.

Although creativity and imagination will be more fully explored in chapter two, it is important to briefly discuss

the importance of creativity in its relationship to desire. Throughout history, people have had the desire to create. The cave paintings at Lascaux from the Paleolithic Era are perhaps the earliest examples of this desire to make something. Images of animals and hunters span the interior walls of the cave in what

1.2 A horse from Lascaux

may have been decoration for the habitation, a celebration of a successful hunt, or a wish for the bison to return from their winter locations. We do not know exactly why these early people felt a desire to draw these images, but the need to leave a physical mark to define and control the environment was obviously very strong even 17,000 years ago.

The inclination to create can stem from a number of reasons, whether it is to find a solution to a particular need, to pursue possible ideas, or simply as a result of some sudden inspiration. The students in Sandra's studio, whether they know it or not, are attempting to stimulate their imaginations, and subsequently their creativity, in various different ways. It is true that creativity does not occur in the absence of stimulus, as mentioned earlier, since it needs to be encouraged through experiences and observations. Soon had been tearing paper into forms and through this seemingly insignificant action, he is able to see unexpected shapes that may spark ideas for potential solutions. John, on the other hand, is exploring design and architecture magazines. By studying published projects by accomplished designers, he is able to identify possible strategies to fit his particular situation. He is not planning to copy the designs exactly, but is trying to understand how their solutions responded to a specific program, site, or particular client. The three students discussing the project may be brainstorming in an attempt to stimulate ideas through tossing abstract concepts back and forth. Tom is piling stools, testing the boundaries of gravity and form. In a similar way, Mike, by turning his model upside down, is providing a unique view that questions norms and provides a different perspective on something he thought was a solution. Madison has been watching the movement of leaves outside the window. The structure and patterns of the leaves may indicate to her a geometry that could be utilized in her design solution.

Each of these students has learned various ways to inspire creativity, but there is also an innate need to create that occurs very early in life. Children learn by manipulating their environment. They will draw with anything they can hold, and on any surface available. They will stack blocks, build with Lego, or make forts out of couch cushions. By stacking blocks, they learn the effects of gravity, and by drawing with crayons, they learn fine motor movement and the beginnings of representation.[3]

1.3 Child playing with unit blocks

Architects, artists, and designers also have an innate need to create. They use media to find solutions to issues, but they also make images and models to represent what they see, visualize something unseen, work through a discovery, evaluate a proposal, record an idea or dream so that it is not forgotten, or they may just have an uncontrollable urge to create. The choir of the Gothic church of Saint Denis outside of Paris, France is an example of an urge to create.

The desire for a light-filled sacred space was resolved with the development of tall walls opened with large pointed arch windows and supported by external buttresses. The development of these elements tested the possibilities of architectural technology of the time. Both the desire for an impressive light-filled space that evoked the presence of God and the need for the technical solution marked the beginning of the Gothic period.

Beyond a solution to a specific challenge, the need to create can also result from a sudden urge or inspiration. An episode of *The Simpsons* parodied the American architect Frank Gehry crumpling a piece of paper and being suddenly inspired for the design of a concert hall.[4] Obviously Frank Gehry is an architect continually thinking about constructing buildings, but the scenario suggested that the crumpled paper stimulated an instantaneous

1.4 Guggenheim Museum, Frank Gehry

Beginning

connection in his mind for a potential structure. Similar to the writings of the author Italo Calvino, much of creativity is finding unusual connections between seemingly unrelated things.[5]

Although inspiration will be further explored in chapter two, learning to be creative is primarily concerned with learning a new process of thinking. This process is never completely clear, nor does anyone know how it will turn out. It is common for architects and designers to feel off-balance when designing, since there is so much uncertainty, and so many unknowns. Creativity is not only the inspiration that happens at the beginning of the process, but also the way designers progress through their thinking to ensure a logical, desirable product. Desire, as a function of seeking perfection and anticipating the future, begins the process, while creativity needs time, patience, and knowing how to pursue inspiration. Ultimately, this creative intent can begin through the interaction with designers' surrounding context and experiences.

SEEING AND EXPERIENCING

To desire is necessary for creation, but how do we know what to desire? For artists, what to make may emerge from wanting to portray a strong emotion, the belief in a political direction, the recognition of a social injustice, or the conveyance of a pastoral scene. For architects and designers, desire may be connected to perceived need, either a directive from a client or social need such as efficiency, shelter, or convenience. For designers to perceive both needs and solutions, they must be knowledgeable about the world and be aware of their surroundings. The author John Berger writes about the relationship between seeing and knowing.

Seeing comes before words. The child looks and recognizes before it can speak. But there is also another sense in which seeing comes before words. It is seeing which establishes our place in the surrounding world; we explain that world with words, but words can never undo the fact that we are surrounded by it. The relation between what we see and what we know is never settled.[6]

It may be easy to *see* but when paired with *understanding* the task is more difficult. Seeing and experiencing are ways to help us understand our environment.

The context that surrounds us is generally accepted as the physical representation of an environment's history,

and the way in which it has accumulated different levels of meaning to form the specific quality of the site. Gottfried Semper, a German architect and author of the *Four Elements of Architecture*, states that "the environment is therefore not a system in which to dissolve architecture. On the contrary, it is the most important material from which to develop the project."[7]

1.5 Architecture student, Victor Kuslikis, from Ryerson University sketching during a trip to Turkey

On the first day of first year studio, Robert's professor takes the entire class on a field trip to a local site. Robert brings his camera, as do all the students. He also has been told to bring his pencils and a new, empty sketchbook. While on the site, the students scour the lot taking photographs from every angle and location. The professor then calls the group together and tells everyone to put away their cameras and cell phones, and to take out their sketchbooks to interpret the site. Robert and his classmates stare at the blank pages of their sketchbooks. But didn't they just document the site? Is not a photo better at capturing details than anything that they could sketch?

The professor explains the purpose of the field trip. The assignment for that studio session is to document, analyze, and interpret the site so that each student can design a small pavilion for an upcoming exhibition. The professor explains that she wants the class to learn about perception and how to understand the context so that they will be able to design an appropriate pavilion. She suggests that they need to observe things on the site that cannot be seen. With this, Robert and his classmates are thoroughly confused. The professor then quotes the architect Louis Kahn who said:

> There is no value in trying to imitate exactly. Photographs will serve you best of all, if that is your aim. We should not imitate when our intention is to create – to improvise ... The capacity to see comes from persistently analyzing our reactions to what we look at, and their significance as far as we are concerned. The more one looks, the more one will come to see.[8]

Robert and his classmates are asked to return to their exploration of the site with the hope that they will perceive what they *see* more clearly.

As a function of desire, learning to be designers and architects means to be naturally curious and discover the best ways to investigate what you do not know. So returning to Robert and his studio, each student needs to learn how to observe, interpret, and understand an environment. A first step would be for the students to take time to concentrate on representing what they see through drawing, but is this enough? Architects and designers also need to understand how to use analysis to assist in comprehending what they see. Analysis includes understanding how the parts of something work together to make a whole.[9] For you, as beginning students of design, this may involve trying to imagine what is below, above, or behind what you are observing. It might include studying the object or site from various viewpoints – from the top of neighboring buildings or lying on the ground. It is important to diagram the most salient features of the environment, which might include tracking pedestrian movements, locating traffic patterns, or drawing sections through the site to understand height relationships. The sound of nature or traffic certainly provides awareness of how a site is perceived. In a like manner, the aromas of the trees, or the feeling of the breeze affects how an environment is understood. It is obvious that these analytical techniques are something other than passive observation.

Experiencing a site or contemplating a design issue, architects and designers should be consciously aware of their senses. Emotions are tied to the taste, sound, feel, and smell of designed objects or architectural spaces. For example, product designers need to consider the texture of objects, how they feel when they are held, and architects must understand the qualities of materials and how sound is absorbed or echoed. Part of understanding the value of human senses involves the emotions that they evoke, and these feelings are difficult to recognize. Acknowledging or projecting emotional or sensory stimulus into design means that designers must first recognize the part they play in perception.

Perception is the way in which something is regarded, understood, or interpreted. The word comes from the Latin verb *percipere*, which means "to seize, or understand."[10] Perception is important in learning about design because it allows designers and architects to better understand what they *see*. The psychologist and philosopher, J.J. Gibson, provides an interesting approach to the structure of the human eye and thus what it means to really see. Unlike physiologists who describe vision as an inverted image reflected on the retina, Gibson suggests that humans see an array of colors and forms that need to be interpreted by the mind.[11] In other words, each person must decipher what they are seeing by matching shapes and colors with what they know of the context around them. This makes a connection between what is seen and how people understand the impressions reflected in their eyes. It also explains how people will *see* what they want to see, and this also expresses how important interpretation and expectation is to the act of vision. The film by the great Japanese film director Akira Kurosawa, *Rashomon* (1950), explored the notion that people will all perceive an incident differently. A crime viewed through the perceptions of several witnesses reveals the various views of what happened. The movie *Kagemusha* (1980), also directed by Kurosawa, studies an impersonator who assumes the persona of a king. The characters in the film expect and want to believe the impersonator is the king, thus his performance is convincing. Any preconceived notions influence what is viewed.

When Robert's class is asked to sketch what they see on the site, their professor is asking them to take an active, rather than passive role in seeing. A photograph will capture a view without being critical, and it will reproduce a composition that is indiscriminate. The professor is asking students to notice elements in the environment that they had never seen before. Those things might be the way shadows fall on a surface, textures found in the environment, or how pedestrian movement over the site creates patterns. Through the observations necessary to draw, designers and students can learn to see the nuances of places and objects. A drawing requires study and reflection to make evident shapes and relationships. In contrast to a camera's simple point-and-shoot, a drawing commands time to execute. This "seeing-to-know" strengthens skills of perception; learning to really look assists designers and architects to see aspects of the world they have never noticed before.

A second aspect involves perception as understanding or "seeing-to-understand." Robert and his classmates do not recognize that the importance of studying a site and its context is to learn about things that are less easy to recognize. To truly comprehend a site or context might mean to spend many days there or return for numerous visits.

The American architect, Antoine Predock, is known for his sensitive architectural responses to the desert in the southwestern United States. He reportedly camps out on a potential site, to see the atmosphere in the morning, feel the dew at dawn, or watch the composition of stars in the night sky. Mr. Predock experiences the site in all its qualities, making sure that he understands the complexities of the environment as a whole.[12]

Architects and designers utilize many techniques to document, study, and analyze an unfamiliar environment. They certainly utilize photography, but they will also look for souvenirs, sketch what they encounter, make notes of what they hear and smell, taste the local foods, and experience the culture. These represent a few techniques that assist designers and architects to interpret an environment. *Interpretation* is the action of explaining the meaning of something. It also pertains to a stylistic representation of a performance.[13] Everything we make has a certain amount of intention that is not always obvious. The author of a book or the designers of objects, for example, are not always available to explain their reasoning. Meaning can be extrapolated from observation, comparison, analysis, and an understanding of past experiences. Much of the study of interpretation stems from the theory of hermeneutics. At its most basic, hermeneutics originated with reference to the mythological Greek god Hermes (and his Roman equivalent Mercury) and is an area of inquiry that deals with interpretation of the Bible or literary texts.[14]

1.6 The Greek god Mercury

Historically scholars and theologians were required to arrive at their own understanding of these texts because the authors were no longer available to explain. People are always trying to find order in chaos, and for designers and architects it is important to attempt to instill logic into the built environment.

You cannot interpret without understanding your intention. You need to decide what is important about your exploration, and you need to ask yourself how this information will help you in your future design. The best way to successfully understand meaning is to judge something against the set of rules governing what you are attempting to do. Such rules, for example, could be based on what you believe, ideals of earlier architects and designers, the laws of basic human nature, or boundaries set by the society that you live in.

Memory also affects the interpretation of things you see and experience. Most people maintain a collection of memories from experiences of places, things, and events. Memory is not only recall but can be an active part of design and intention. The aspect of memory, *memor,* "to be mindful," is critical not as the passive recollection of events but as consciously using memory to engage in a dialogue about design.[15] Being "mindful," for architects, implies working though design, and can enhance the outcome of your projects. Memories of prior experiences act as comparators to help understand new information. Memory retains impressions, but more distinct memories are those accompanied by emotions. For example, people will remember traumatic or frightening experiences with great detail. Memories of senses are also very distinct, for example, the strong aroma of cheese may evoke instantaneous memories of shops in Paris, or the smell of tobacco might remind one of a favorite grandfather. In a like manner, the experience of architectural spaces presents strong emotions. The architecture professor Dr. Julio Bermudez has been documenting examples of buildings that cause an emotional response. One of the buildings that universally moves architects is the Pantheon in Rome. Constructed in the first century AD, it exhibits proportions that can be felt in the volume: the width of the space in contrast to its height. This structure was designed to represent the universe, with a circle inscribed within its section. The oculus in the center

1.7 Interior of the Pantheon, Rome

of the dome recalls the sun in the sky and illuminates the space with gentle continuously moving light. When your professors take you on field trips to visit generally reputable buildings, they are attempting to increase your repertoire of experiences that can be recalled and integrated into your own designs. To preserve memories, architects and designers often record their experiences through drawings and photographs.

When Robert and his studio-mates are confronted with the blank pages in their sketchbooks, they should think about what is important to study when visiting a site. They need to consider all aspects of their intentions and how best to explore, call upon their memories and experiences, and analyze the information they can find. The blank page should not be seen as something worrisome but an opportunity to relay experiences and desires. If Robert and his classmates are expected to consider their own experiences and learn to relate these experiences and memories when contemplating intent, then it is important to consider experience as a relationship between the human body and the space of experience.

Architectural theorists studying phenomenology discuss that a body "simultaneously sees and is seen. That which looks at all things can also look at itself and recognize, in that it sees, the 'other side' of its power of looking. It sees itself seeing; it touches itself touching; it is visible and sensitive for itself."[16] People are aware of their bodies and thus aware of their bodies in space. Architecture defines itself as a mediator between the body and its environment, acting as shelter and protection, or a second skin. For example, this may be why it has been argued that there is a direct connection between the origins of architecture and dance, since both deal with the body in space and rituals or habits of how we try to control nature.[17]

The body has long been used as an analogy for buildings. For example, architects have designed cathedrals whose floor plans reflect the proportions of the human body. In addition to architecture, many concepts of space, time, and numbers were generated from the human body. The square, the four cardinal directions, and the four seasons, derive from the four directions of our bodies. Since Greek antiquity, the human body has been regarded as a microcosm of universal harmony. The Greek philosopher Protagoras wrote, "Man is the measure of all things, of things that are, that they are; and of things that are not, that they are not."[18] Babies learn to understand scale and the world around them through their bodies. They grab their feet, the bars of their cribs, or their mother's fingers and through this interaction they learn to measure and interpret. Similarly, Babylonian and Egyptian architects employed units of measurement extracted from the length of arms, hands, and fingers. They passed these traditions to the Greeks and Romans, creating units of measure such as the cubit. Even today, people use the body as a way to explain the world through icons and symbols, such as measuring in feet. For the built environment, the relationship between the body and architecture has long been a topic of interest. Vitruvius in his treatise *The Ten Books of Architecture* writes that the proportions initially adopted for temples and columns were based on the human body, as an accepted model of strength and beauty. In his view, proportion is a correspondence between the measures of the members of an entire work and of the whole, to a certain part selected as standard.[19] In like manner, measurement, around the world, reflects a reference standard of the human body. "Architecture is our primary instrument in relating us with space and time, and giving these dimensions a human measure."[20] The understanding of architectural scale involves the constant awareness of the building in relationship to our bodies. When looking at walls and ceilings, for example, we may be subconsciously measuring the space between us and the limits of architectural space.

There is a modern belief that "every fiber of our bodies, every cell of our brains, holds memories."[21] More than a biological explanation, this seems to be a notion that memories are the conduit of knowledge and subsequently all knowledge is based on the foundation of memory. "The whole body is involved in the act of memory, since memory, and especially body memory, is *a-priori*, constantly at work, never inoperative."[22] This interpretation by philosopher Edward Casey seems to suggest something between subconscious intention and instinct, because often actions do not fit into a mentally remembered place or that which is purely intuitive. Body memory is "intrinsic to the body, its own ways of remembering: how we remember in and by and through the body."[23]

Architectural experience utilizes smell, taste, touch, sight, and sound as we are continually interacting with our environment. Phenomenology, particularly in architecture, involves the experience of spaces and building materials, and focuses on their sensory qualities. Contemporary architects such as Steven Holl, Peter Zumthor, and Tado Andao have concentrated on inhabitants' perceptions of architectural space. They utilize tactile materials, the sharpness or softness of light and materials that either reflect or dampen sound, for example. The architect and theorist, Juhani Pallasmaa, has written several books questioning the human body in relationship to architecture and sensory experience and writes that, "All the senses, including vision, are extensions of the tactile sense; the senses are specialisations of skin tissue, and all sensory experiences are modes of touching and thus related to tactility."[24]

Other theorists, over the last several decades, have explored an interpretation of "body" as deconstructed. In an investigation of the postmodern body based on the psycho-analyst Sigmund Freud's concept of the *uncanny*, Anthony Vidler writes of the human body in fragments and the disturbing loss of the "integrated body." In other words, postmodern theory relates that this fragmentation, and the notion of constant reflection, shows how humanist progress is in disorder.[25]

Ultimately, architecture is about making spaces to protect and inspire people. The boundaries of this space are like a second skin, and how our bodies inhabit this volume affects how we perceive buildings. As a student, you should be aware of how the human body is a way to understand scale, and design for how people experience space.

DESIRING

The term *desire* comes from the Latin *desiderare* meaning "to long for, wish for, demand or expect." Originally the term came from *de sidere*, which literally means "from the stars." This heavenly origin linked desire intimately to the gods and, thus, perfection. The definition of desire philosophically has been a cause of debate and controversy for many years. Most commonly, *desire* has been connected with *belief* in order to "explain a voluntary or intentional action" taken by an individual. A desire to achieve something is related to the belief that the choice of action will ultimately lead to this goal.[26] The ancient Greek philosopher Plato thought of desire as tied to the term *eros* (love), but more interesting, desire could be seen as a combination of *logistikon* (the capacity to think things through) and *philomathes* (lover of learning).[27] Thus, desire and reason are directly related to most actions we, as people, take.

Another Greek philosopher, Aristotle, on the other hand, believed that a thought or an idea "by itself ... moves nothing," unless it is attached to desire.[28] Tied to what he described as assets of character (the non-rational part of people) and to the positive qualities of intellect (the rational part), the desires for a proper outcome depend upon a person's morals and beliefs coupled with their knowledge.[29] Both Plato's and Aristotle's ideas on desire point out the most important reason for its existence – change. Without having the desire to achieve something, we cannot even begin to think of changing or bettering the world around us.

Jean-Jacques Rousseau, most known for his philosophical impact on the Enlightenment and the French Revolution, also explored the role of desire in the ways we think about ourselves, especially in relationship to society and politics.[30] He believed that desire is innately tied to the individual – it is constantly at center stage, whether for better or worse, always searching for unity or community.[31] For the French philosopher Gilles Deleuze, desire is related to constructing a collection of things,[32] thus suggesting that desire is the construction equating action and change. As people we are wired to desire, to want, to need – it is within our chemical makeup, it is what keeps our civilization in constant movement and why we are continually trying to innovate. For design, desire is what changes an idea or a project, it is the reason for the idea from the beginning. Designers have the desire for creativity and thus, the urge to create.[33] Without desire we would no longer feel the need to create or to make changes in our built environment.

For example, Kevin, as a first year architecture student, receives the outline for an assignment from his studio professor. The project calls for a gateway design based upon one of the imagined cities from Italo Calvino's book *Invisible Cities*. As he reads the passage he becomes quite excited with the possibilities it entails. His mind reels with ideas and he can't wait to begin the assignment. The feeling that Kevin is experiencing is desire – he desires creativity and is urged to create the designs for the gateway. Without this desire, Kevin would neither wish to design the project nor have any excitement about reading the passage.

Similarly, firms such as Archigram and Superstudio from the 1960s and 1970s produced work that seemed highly unlikely and unrealistic yet had a great impact on the profession. Their designs were futuristic mega-structures and walking cities that attacked the bleak and uninspired profession of architecture at the time.[34] These avant-garde architects relished in the glory of designing limitlessly, since their designs were not constrained by build-ability, budget, clients, or property laws. This provided them the freedom to create these graphic social commentaries that were unsettling to the society and culture of their time. And further still, in their most influential form, students and young architects studied their drawings and eventually sought to pursue some of those radical ideas in the built form. Their desire to create these drawings, and the critique of the context they experienced, caused change in the profession and impacted design thereafter. Desire is needed to begin a project, to want to accomplish and create something, but as these firms have shown us, desire is also needed on a higher level. It is not just enough to desire to create, but we must desire to create something meaningful, powerful, pleasing, and specifically something that is ultimately worthwhile.

DEVELOPING A POSITION

After a semester studying the architecture of Neoclassicism, Ben decides to model his studio project after some of the principles of the architect Claude-Nicolas Ledoux. However, when explaining his inspiration, his instructor has some suggestions. "While looking to precedent found in past buildings is good, you should consider that the principles of the 1700s worked for that particular time period, the issues of today are very different, and require a different approach and intent." Ben's instructor also notes that she doesn't see any of Ben's own personal views in the project. She suggests that much like creating a *parti* for a particular project, Ben should reflect on what he wants his designs to promote and make sure that they are relevant for today.

Defined as "a proposition or thesis laid down or stated … a belief, or opinion,"[35] an architectural position is something that evolves over time and may not fully form until an architect has entered professional practice. A position may also continue to morph as architects gain new experiences and the world around them changes. It is important to understand the factors that can influence an architectural position and begin to think about which ones are most important to pursue.

Although in professional practice an architectural project is ultimately initiated by a client's wishes, architects bring with them a distinct set of factors that influence how they approach design and what they want architecture to convey. These past experiences and beliefs that each person has learned from and grown to support, influence how they design, even if they may not be aware of it. An architect who has had the chance to travel and experience different cultures will have a different approach to design than one who has lived in a small town their entire life.

1.8 Barcelona Pavilion, Mies van der Rohe

For example, one person might design with privacy in mind while another may design to encourage a sense of community. This is not to say that one approach is necessarily better than another, but it is important to note that there are many wide-ranging views on what is most important in a design.

Zeitgeist, defined as "the spirit or genius, which marks the thought or feeling of a period or age,"[36] is another important influence for architectural practice. While it may not be apparent until years later, the particular worldview of a time heavily influences design. As the modern architect Ludwig Mies van der Rohe declared, "architecture is the will of an epoch translated into space,"[37] and an architect of a particular time will bring this influence into design. For example, in the 1950s, the idea of home ownership and the American dream led to the development of suburbia, and the mass-produced architecture of that period. While today we may have a different interpretation of the suburbs, the zeitgeist of the mid-twentieth century was quite different. The adoption of a position indicates the desire to fulfill certain ideals, whether it is the rational thought of ancient Greece, or the religious piety of the Renaissance. Both of these ideals influenced the architecture of the time with the former promoting highly formalized structure, and the latter highly ornamented and grand buildings. Ideals, whether personal or shared by a society, provide the framework through which desire can be channeled.

While for many students an architectural position may seem like something reserved for architectural celebrities or well-established practitioners, having a position, or at least beginning to develop one, is important to consider. Architecture is unique in that it is something that all people interact with on a daily basis, whether or not they are aware of it. It is also something that is incredibly enduring and has the ability to influence how people live for decades after it has been built. Having a position towards design therefore is of the utmost importance because of the influence that architecture can have on its context and the people who reside in it. There are far too many buildings that have been built with no thought of how they will affect the environment in which they have been created, nor the people who have to live in or around them. To infuse meaning into a building, no matter how small or seemingly insignificant, an architectural position ensures that architecture has a purpose beyond simply providing shelter. As Paul Goldberger writes, "Architecture begins to matter when it goes beyond protecting us from the elements, when it begins to say something about the world."[38]

Architecture's ability to influence not only current, but also future populations suggests that an architectural position inevitably requires the discussion of responsibility. Because of the impact of architecture on the environment, economy, and social structure of a community, an architect's position requires careful consideration. For example, the current state of the environment has created a push for sustainable, "green" architecture. An architect's responsibility towards the environment is something that must be incorporated into their architectural position as climate change and diminishing resources become more of a concern. Similarly, the responsibility for the needs of a society can heavily influence an architect. For example, the modern architect Le Corbusier stated that "it is a question of building which is at the root of the social unrest of today," noting the poor living conditions that many people faced in crowded cities in the 1920s.[39] Subsequently, his architectural position strongly advocated for green space and a division of living and working spaces that can be seen throughout much of his work.

While the desire to create is strong for architects, they must mediate this desire through a careful consideration of the effects that their work can have. Being aware of the various influences that architecture can have, the influences that the current state of the world has on architecture, and using these factors to develop a position can bring focus to each project.

BALANCING

Stephanie starts working on a new project to build a studio for a violinist. Eager to show how innovative she can be, she comes up with a radical new form for the building and creates beautiful, evocative renderings to capture her concept. During the final critique, however, a visiting musician points out that the shape of the building would create very poor acoustical conditions for the high pitch notes of a violin. In her effort to express her own talent, Stephanie forgot to balance her desire to create something interesting with the need for it to be useful.

Balance is the state of "stability or steadiness due to the equilibrium prevailing between all the forces of any system,"[40] and is an integral skill to learn in design. As a person walking a tightrope would most definitely understand, leaning to one side or another too far can be a dangerous thing, and whether it is mediating between the needs of a client and your own views, or the balance between aesthetics and function, straying too far to one side or the other can have equally negative repercussions.

Balance has an important place within design because it not only refers to external forces on a product, such as the views of the client and designer, but it also occurs internally within a design. Vitruvius described architecture as the balance between *firmitas*, *utilitas*, and *venustas* (firmness, commodity, and delight). He stated that:

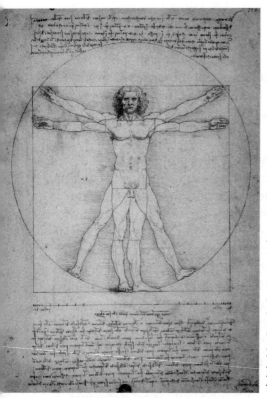

1.9 *Vitruvian Man*, Leonardo Da Vinci

"durability will be assured when foundations are carried down to the solid ground and materials wisely and liberally selected; convenience, when the arrangement of the apartments is faultless and presents no hindrance to use, and when each class of building is assigned to its suitable and appropriate exposure; and beauty, when the appearance of the work is pleasing and in good taste, and when its members are in due proportion according to correct principles of symmetry."[41]

According to Vitruvius, architecture does not exist without the presence of all three of these components, and only when they are in equal measure, without the domination of any single attribute. In his seminal work *Ten Books of Architecture*, Vitruvius writes of temples' dependence upon symmetry and proportion. He states, "without symmetry and proportion there can be no principles in the design of any temple; that is, if there is no precise relation between its members, as in the case of those of a well shaped man."[42]

This description of the body of a man was later illustrated as the early Renaissance artist, inventor, and architect, Leonardo Da Vinci's *Vitruvian Man*. This drawing showing a man circumscribed within a circle and a square, arms and legs touching the edges, thus revealed the proportions of an ideal human male. Beyond the scientific or anthropological aspects of the work, there are deeper symbolic meanings within it. The image of a man circumscribed within a circle is a medieval representation of how humans were viewed as the center of the universe, and as a microcosm of it. The man is proportionally balanced and he is also in balance with the universe.[43] The image itself, in its portrayal of the mathematical proportions of the body, as well as the inclusion of the spiritual aspect of the human's place in the universe, demonstrates the essential balance that is aimed for in every work. As the essence of a "Renaissance Man," Da Vinci understood the message of balance; he was able to strike a balance between the arts and sciences, gaining a broad expertise in each discipline. He is known for his paintings, military fortification designs, architectural conceptions, technological inventions, and anatomical explorations.

There are many examples of architecture that is imbalanced in some regard. For example, one of the current

trends in architecture is computational design and digital fabrication in the construction process. Architects have found that they are able to become closer to the building process through computation, and as such, are able to design much more complex buildings. Some may argue that this leads to "form for form's sake": building something complex because you are now able to. Architecture as well as design has many aspects that must be balanced, and being too focused on one aspect becomes detrimental to the others. For example, in Daniel Libeskind's Royal Ontario

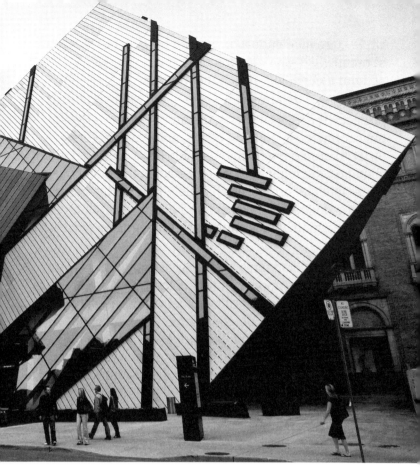

1.10 The Royal Ontario Museum Crystal, Daniel Libeskind

Museum in Toronto, the focus was the complexity of the construction, and the iconic form of the building. However, these forms also created difficult spaces in which to display specimens. The essential function of the museum, the ability to display objects, was compromised for a unique form. Christine M. Piotrowski, author of *Problem Solving and Critical Thinking for Designers*, argues that this type of thinking begins in schools, where "students have an especially difficult time understanding that design, while a creative endeavor, is not a personal expression of creativity."[44] She reminds us that it is difficult to design without a client to balance the process.

In design, synthesis is the balancing of the inputs of the project – the client's needs, the architect's own design philosophy, cost, building codes, and other factors – in order to create the optimum result. Each factor is carefully managed to create a harmony between the pieces, and a more dynamic project. By balancing the architect's desires with the desires of the client and other constraints, the result is a more successful project that comes closest to an ideal.

For Robert, Stephanie, and their classmates, this is a vital lesson. It is important to recognize that architecture and design are collaborative endeavors. There are many influences that must be considered in the inception of a project and throughout the process of design and construction. The participants (programmers, structural engineers, lighting consultants, and many others) must all work together to make a successful building. Architects would not be successful if they discounted the needs of their clients, although it is imperative to remember that you will be the trained professional, so your opinion is important.

The desire to create is an urge that starts early in life, and for designers only gets stronger with time. Our desire to create inspires us to look for solutions to perceived needs and pursue possibilities that others may not see or understand. This type of awareness is something that must be learned through careful observation of our surroundings and the perception of our senses. It is influenced by your life experiences, what you believe, and your thoughts concerning design to such an extent that you should begin to develop your own outlook on what constitutes an ideal design. What each designer must keep in mind, however, is that your desire to create must be balanced with the desires of others, and, as you most likely have already noticed, design and architecture are inherently collaborative. Each person who interacts with design, whether directly or indirectly, brings with them their own set of experiences and ideals, and it is only through careful consideration of each side that harmony can be achieved. Design, and learning in turn, is never linear, and requires a combination of looking both back on what has been learned and forward to what could be, to become truly successful.

The urge to create is certainly a feeling that is shared by all designers, but when faced with a specific issue that needs resolution, we often find ourselves at a loss for inspiration. Much like Sandra, who found herself sitting in the studio late at night without any ideas, inspiration is sometimes hard to come by. The difficulty in having so many forces to balance is that the problem becomes overwhelming and we find ourselves stumped. But as Sandra saw by observing her fellow students manipulating materials, brainstorming together, or looking to precedents, there are many ways that we can kindle the spark of inspiration.

Endnotes

1   *The Compact Edition of the Oxford English Dictionary* (Oxford: Oxford University Press, 1971), s.v. "create."

2   Although a common adage of the time, this saying has been attributed to Thomas Edison, and it appears that a version of it was published in the *Chicago Tribune* in 1904.

3   Laura E. Berk, *Infants and Children*, 5th ed. (Boston: Pearson Education, 2005), 347.

4   Matt Groening, "The Seven-Beer Snitch," *The Simpsons*, season 16, episode 14, directed by Matthew Nastuk (Burbank, CA: FOX, 2005), television.

5   Italo Calvino, *Six Memos for the Next Millennium* (Cambridge, MA: Harvard University Press, 1988), 42–45.

6   John Berger, *Ways of Seeing* (London: Penguin Books, 1972), 7.

7   See Kenneth Frampton, "Rappel à l'Ordre: The Case for the Tectonic," in *Labour, Work and Architecture: Collected Essays on Architecture and Design* (London: Phaidon Press, 2002), 27–28.

8   Louis I. Kahn, *Writings, Lectures, Interviews*, ed. Alessandra Latour (New York: Rizzoli, 1991), 11.

9   *Oxford English Dictionary*, s.v. "analysis."

10 Ibid., s.v. "perception."

11 James J. Gibson, *Reasons for Realism: Selected Essays of James J. Gibson*, eds. Edward Reed and Rebecca Jones (New Jersey: Lawrence Erlbaum Associates, 1982), 261.

12 From a lecture by Antoine Predock at the ACSA Annual Meeting in New Orleans, March 1986.

13 *Oxford English Dictionary*, s.v. "interpretation."

14 For more on hermeneutics see Hans-Georg Gadamer, *Truth and Method* (New York: Crossroads, 1989) or Dalibor Vesely, *Architecture in the Age of Divided Representation: The Question of Creativity in the Shadow of Production* (Cambridge, MA: MIT Press, 2004).

15 *Oxford English Dictionary*, s.v. "memory."

16 Edward S. Casey, *Remembering: A Phenomenological Study* (Bloomington: Indiana University Press, 1987), 18.

17 Maurice Merleau-Ponty, *The Primacy of Perception*, ed. James M. Edie (Evanston: Northwestern University Press 1964), 162.

18 Richard Padovan, *Proportion: Science, Philosophy, Architecture* (London: E&FN Spon, 1999), 5.

19 Vitruvius, *On Architecture*, trans. Frank Granger (Cambridge, MA: Harvard University Press, 2002), 159–167.

20 Juhani Pallasmaa, *Eyes of the Skin: Architecture and the Senses* (New Jersey: John Wiley and Sons, 2005), 17.

21 Casey, *Remembering*, ix.

22 Ibid., 146–147.

23 Ibid., 147.

24 Pallasmaa, *Eyes of the Skin*, 10.

25 See Anthony Vidler, *The Architectural Uncanny* (Cambridge, MA: MIT Press, 1994).

26 *Oxford English Dictionary*, s.v. "desire."

27 Charles H. Kahn, "Plato's Theory of Desire," *The Review of Metaphysics*, no. 1 (September 1987): 82.

28 T. H. Irwin, "Aristotle on Reason, Desire, and Virtue," *The Journal of Philosophy*, no. 17 (October 2, 1975): 567.

29 Ibid., 569.

30 Mark Blackell, John Duncan, and Simon Kow, eds. *Rousseau and Desire* (Toronto: University of Toronto Press, 2009), 3.

31 Ibid., 4.

32 Peter Blundell Jones, Doina Petrescu, and Jeremy Till, eds, *Architecture and Participation* (New York: Spon Press, 2005), 45.

33 Henrietta Palmer, "Desire," in *Crucial Words: Conditions for Contemporary Architecture*, eds. Gert Wingårdh and Rasmus Wærn (Boston: Birkhäuser Architecture, 2008), 56.

34 See, for example, Nicolai Ouroussoff, "An Architect Unshackled by Limits of the Real World." *New York Times*, www.nytimes.com/2008/08/25/arts/design/25wood.html?pagewanted=all&_r=0.

35 *Oxford English Dictionary*, s.v. "position."

36 Ibid., s.v. "zeitgeist."

37 John Zukowsky, *Mies Reconsidered: His Career, Legacy, and Disciples* (New York: Rizzoli, 1986), 17.

38 Paul Goldberger, *Why Architecture Matters* (New Haven: Yale University Press, 2009), ix.

39 Le Corbusier, *Towards a New Architecture*, trans. Frederick Etchells (New York: Dover Publications, 1986), 269.

40 *Oxford English Dictionary*, s.v. "balance."

41 Vitruvius, translated by Morris Hicky Morgan, *The Ten Books on Architecture* (Cambridge, MA: Harvard University Press and London: Humphrey Milford/Oxford University Press, 1914), 17.

42 Ibid., 73.

43 For the human body is so designed by nature that the face, from the chin to the top of the forehead and the lowest roots of the hair, is a tenth part of the whole height; the open hand from the wrist to the tip of the middle finger is just the same; the head from the chin to the crown is an eighth, and with the neck and shoulder from the top of the breast to the lowest roots of the hair is a sixth; from the middle of the breast to the summit of the crown is a fourth. If we take the height of the face itself, the distance from the bottom of the chin to the under side of the nostrils is one third of it; the nose from the under side of the nostrils to a line between the eyebrows is the same; from there to the lowest roots of the hair is also a third, comprising the forehead. The length of the foot is one sixth of the height of the body; of the forearm, one fourth; and the breadth of the breast is also one fourth. The other members, too, have their own symmetrical proportions, and it was by employing them that the famous painters and sculptors of antiquity attained to great and endless renown.

Martin Germ, "Leonardo's Vitruvian Man, Renaissance Humanism, and Nicholas of Cus," *Art (Prague)* 55, no. 2 (2007): 102–107.

44 Christine M. Piotrowski, *Problem Solving and Critical Thinking for Designers* (New Jersey: Wiley, 2011), 19.

Imagining

Chapter 2

Design is a plan for
arranging elements
in such a way as best
to accomplish a
particular purpose.

Charles Eames

Chapter one discussed the desire that motivates people to build, design, or make, in an effort to identify why architects and designers are drawn to the discipline. It also discussed the balance necessary for successful architecture. This chapter explores how to use your imagination to find a strong concept that will guide your design through the process of development.

An architectural or design concept is a guiding principle that gives a project direction. It is the theme of the project, the argument, or big idea that guides such elements as order, proportions, organization, or hierarchy, and is often determined by the most important aspects that the project must accomplish. These priorities are the boundaries that guide designers, and are important because designers need to establish limits as to what should and should not be considered. Without this guidance anything is possible and judgment becomes impossible. It is important to identify your priorities so that you can design accordingly.

The site, client needs, ecological environment, efficiency, context, or even an abstract idea or poem could all stimulate a concept, but getting an initial idea is not an easy task. How can you spark imagination? Where do ideas even come from? And how can you tell if your idea is good once you have one? All of these questions will be discussed in the following chapter. Let us begin with a brief exploration of imagination and related issues.

CALLING UPON THE MUSES

Jason, after being accepted to a program in architecture, is starting to wonder if he has what it takes to make it in design. When he was younger, he was always told that he was creative when he drew pictures of made up monsters or ran around the house pretending to be a superhero, but architecture school is more than just whimsy. Can he learn to engage his imagination to design effectively?

As stated previously, some people seem to have a greater propensity for creative acts than others. It is convincing to say that some have a natural talent for design or they seem to have a heightened awareness of intuition. This may be true, but more likely, some individuals have learned how to access their creative potentialities or have, through experience, found ways to more easily draw them forward into action. This is what design studio is about. Part of the reason that there are so many different projects in studio, instead of just learning to design a single building, is that students need to repeatedly practice the process of design, and projects often build upon each other, becoming continually more complex. In early architectural studios, students may be assigned the design of a simple entrance, while in upper years, students may be given the project of a complex building including mechanical systems, structure, parking, and many spaces of different uses. Larger buildings are not necessarily more difficult to design, but they do have more elements to consider. The famous American architect Philip Johnson once said that the hardest things to design are chairs, stairs, and city squares,[1] because in a project with fewer components each part holds more significance.

There are many approaches to design, all equally valid, and there is not one method that works best for everyone. Some of these approaches will be discussed in this chapter and, although not exhaustive, are not to be considered formulaic or definitive. Architects and designers may approach each project from a different direction or with a different method. For example, they may look to brainstorming, word association, metaphors, or analogies as techniques to stimulate their imaginations. What constitutes our imagination is difficult to define, and although it has been studied extensively, it is still not completely understood.

So where to begin? Stories from ancient Greek mythology tell how people who wanted to stimulate their creativity typically began by first calling upon the Muses. The Muses were the daughters of the god Zeus and were goddesses of literature and the arts. With their

2.1 Muses and poets, sarcophagus relief

wealth of knowledge they became the inspiration of poets, artists, authors, and architects, imparting knowledge and acting as spiritual advisors.[2] In contemporary society we still refer to the Muses when looking for artistic inspiration. Authors and artists now use the term as an analogy for people or objects that inspire them to think more broadly or creatively. The word *museum* also has its roots with the Muses, suggesting that knowledge is the basis of inspiration. Sitting and hoping it will occur is never successful, instead it is important to seek experiences and information that will stimulate new ideas. This also means that there is always a period of gestation when the mind must ruminate and ponder. This period is the search for a conceptual beginning and it must be approached actively rather than with passive detachment.

There are three common words used interchangeably to express inventing or finding new ideas: *creation*, *inspiration*, and *imagination*. Through history they have not always meant the same thing, but today we seldom differentiate between them. *Creation* originated from "to make, or produce."[3] Having a relationship to the bringing of something into existence by divine power, *creation* implies something that is brought into being or to form something where nothing was before. In using the term *create* or *creation*, the implication is the act of making something completely new.

The word *inspiration* suggests an awakening of some feeling or impulse. *Inspire* means "to breath in or infuse into the mind or soul."[4] As the opposite of *expire* it implies "to bring to life." Also connected to the divine, it has been used to express the influence of the spirit of God upon the human mind or soul. The word *inspiration* has connotations of bringing something into the mind that has been suggested or prompted.

Imagining

The word *imagination* stems from the formulation of images. To imagine is to form a mental image of something or to represent something in the mind. It also means "to consider, ponder or mediate as part of a thinking process or to make a conjecture, or guess."[5] Philosophers and physiologists have long speculated on the faculties of the imagination, and a further discussion will suggest some of these theories, but it is important to use the term *imagine* in relation to images formed in the mind.

We are constantly using our imaginations. The philosopher Edward Casey writes that it is something easy to engage and we can imagine whatever and however we would like. If the suggestion is made to imagine an elephant, it is quite easy to do. This ability has fascinated philosophers through history, and Aristotle felt that humans think in terms of images.[6] Certainly, today it is accepted that part of our thinking is spatial or object imaging. For the eighteenth-century philosophers David Hume and Immanuel Kant, the imagination had strong representational powers since we can form images, ideas, or likenesses in the mind that help us perceive and interpret the world around us. It is a faculty in addition to our senses because we can form images for ourselves.[7] Casey suggested that the main functions of the imagination are to envisage objects which are absent from our view (such as using our memories or envisaging the elephant), to change or interpret information that we can observe (such as analysis or combining images to make new things, like a unicorn) or to recognize and reuse items that we know (such as knowing the face we see is our mother).[8] Casey presents several properties of the imagination. He writes that it can be both spontaneous and also controlled. In other words, we are often surprised by the sudden influx of associative images that flood our minds, but we can also control what we imagine by deciding to do so.[9] He also identifies that humans limit what they imagine by concentrating on specifics, and that inconsistency does not matter. For example, we can imagine only a specific element, such as the elephant without its context, and in our imaginations it does not matter if the edges are not defined; thus mental impressions are often fuzzy.[10] The images that appear in our imagination are often vague, and if we try to view them more clearly, they seem to disappear. Like dreams, they are often impressions and not entirely vivid. Imagination also lets us assume anything is possible, and in our minds we are not restricted by practicality.[11]

But designers should be cautious of illusion because the imagination can be easily fooled by false images. Gorgeous architectural renderings can often lead us to believe something that is not true. Designers must be able to look beneath the outward appearance of images and understand if the project is true and good. Allusion, on the other hand, is an implied or indirect reference, metaphor, or allegory that can be useful in design. Suggestive and abstract images may hold our attention longer than clear representations, and keep us thinking about their meaning, a key element of a successful concept.

Now that we know something about imagination, how can this information help to find successful concepts? In chapter one, we talked about intention and the decisions and desire to influence the material world through design. *Intent* is the direction of an action toward a goal. Intentionality anticipates the future and thus is a form of imagination – we are imagining a future.[12] We may be able to identify the goal but are not sure how to reach it. Sometimes it is possible to find a concept through rational means (such as logical reasoning) and other times arrival at a concept is found through subconscious means. You can intensify your imagination by intuitively or unintentionally helping your brain to construct images; you can learn to stimulate the parts of your brain that deal with visual things. This might involve metaphors (the transfer of meaning between dissimilar things), and the search for the unusual connections between things. Since our minds are constantly trying to make sense of what we perceive, things that are clear, combined with things that are ambiguous, often expand the imagination.[13] You can also use empathetic imagination as a metaphor. To put yourself in the mind of others, in different scenarios, or in the place of inanimate objects helps find ideas. Stimulating your mind makes things happen. Ideas often come to you when you first awake, or in the shower, this is because you have been thinking about many things, and when your mind is at rest or distracted, they all come together and make sense with an idea or concept.

When beginning to design, the architect Michael Rotondi often draws abstract and associative images to spark his imagination that he calls idea-grams. These drawings give him time to think and concentrate, since one image or line turns into another as he draws whatever comes into his mind. These meditative sketches may not reveal what the design for the

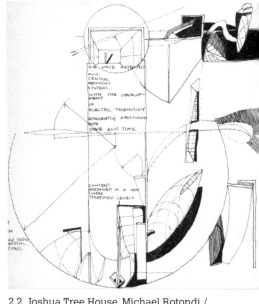

2.2 Joshua Tree House, Michael Rotondi / RoTo Architects

project will look like, but they become a way to use the connection between his hand and his eyes to enhance his memory and evoke imaginative relationships. Although the way that Rotondi designs is unique to his approach, most architects have developed their own processes to stimulate imagination. So, since it is difficult to image anything totally new, designers often begin by recombining things they have seen or experienced, and like the museum of the Muses, they educate themselves in all aspects of the proposed project. Part of this education is to look to the past and the future.

LOOKING BACK AND LOOKING FORWARD

Devon sits at his desk listening to music while trying to think of a concept for the project he has been assigned, a new library for a local neighborhood. He has always liked libraries, ever since he was a child, and used to pretend that the stacks were the corridors of a castle as he read about dragons and knights. His studio instructor has suggested that he look at previous library designs for inspiration, but to also think about future interpretations of the library, when technology might have a greater role. Frustrated by the contradictory advice, Devon leans back in his chair and listens to his music, a playlist of mashups he got from his roommate. He can pick out a number of snippets from familiar songs, both current and old, but remixed together to the same beat they become something completely new and different.

Knowledge of history is essential to architectural education and practice, since the demonstration of knowledge concerning canons and traditions is a part of architectural accreditation and also critical to learning about design.[14] The use of precedent in design has a long history, and as Robert Venturi states, "creating the new for the artist may mean choosing the old."[15] However, architects must also be aware of current trends and prepare for the events of the future. The Italian architect Antonio Sant'Elia is a figure who took this lesson to heart. Born in 1888, he was central to the Futurist movement in Italy and his unrealized designs envisioned a future involving the newest technology of the times.

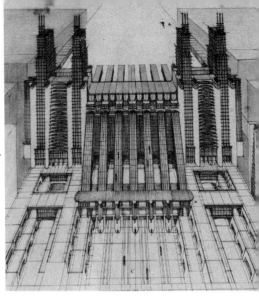

2.3 Air and train station with funicular cableways on three road levels, Antonio Sant'Elia

All architectural students take architectural history courses, learning about the classical orders of the Greeks, the villas of the Renaissance, and the minimalist houses of the Modernists. While some students see these classes as tiresome lectures required only for a credit to graduate, the knowledge of history and precedent is essential to design. "History should form students before they can start to form objects,"[16] as Maurizio Sabini states, suggesting the importance of history to the student of architecture in two major ways. First, most students have experienced architecture in very formative ways even before they enter architecture school. Whether they are aware of it or not, these memories shape the way they see the world, and how they design. Memories of lying on the ground as a child and looking up at the space created by the surrounding trees, or a special reading nook that made them feel content, can have a significant impact on the way that students approach design.

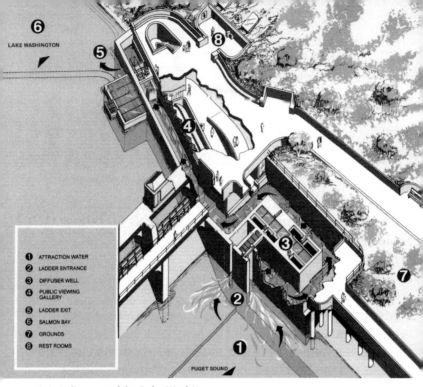

2.4 A diagram of the Lake Washington Ship Canal Fish Ladder

History also shapes students through the study of precedent. *Precedent* in architecture is a "previous solution to a given design problem, usually similar in terms of program, but often situated in a different context."[17] This typically involves the research of existing designs and subsequent analysis to discover the essential characteristics of the structure. The book *Precedents in Architecture: Analytic Diagrams, Formative Ideas, and Partis* by Roger H. Clark and Michael Pause demonstrates the types of analysis typically undertaken in regards to elements such as structure, massing, circulation, symmetry, and balance. The authors also make an important point in the study of precedent:

Our concern is for a continuous tradition that makes the past part of the present. We do not wish to aid the repetition or revival of style whether in whole or part. Rather, by conscious sense of precedent that identifies patterns and themes, we can hope to pursue archetypal ideas that might aid in the generation of architectural form.[18]

The use of precedent is not simply the cutting and pasting of elements to make a new building. Although a building may have a similar program, other elements that went into the building's conception are likely quite different. This means that although you can learn from previous designers' solutions, no two buildings contain all the same variables, and a direct copy is never an acceptable solution. However, using precedent for key, timeless ideas, such as fundamental design principles or basic architectural elements, can be useful when developing a concept early in the design process.

If precedent is such an integral part of architectural design, can we ever really have an original idea? In 2003 when David Childs of Skidmore, Owings & Merrill unveiled the design for the Freedom Tower at ground zero, architect Thomas Shine accused him of plagiarism, taking the matter to court.[19] While imitation in architecture

2.5 Freedom Tower under construction

is certainly not new, the ability to copyright a building was only introduced in 1990.[20] The majority of architects realize that while blatant plagiarism is not encouraged, it is extremely difficult to come up with an entirely new idea in a discipline as old as architecture. Many highly regarded buildings were modeled on other structures, such as Thomas Jefferson's University of Virginia, which imported the classical traditions found in the work of Palladio. Most architects are aware that some aspects of every design will reflect outside influences. Mies van der Rohe even went so far as to say, "I don't want to be original, I just want to be good."

It is almost impossible to create anything entirely new. Most of our dreams and imaginings are based on images or memories that we have seen before, although they may be rearranged into a collection of borrowed parts.[21] Consider a unicorn for example. While the actual animal does not exist, it is a combination of a horse and a horn, two things that we are already familiar with. The key is to take a collection of elements and remix them into something new. The mashups that Devon was listening to are an example of taking disparate sources and reimagining them. They "rely on a deep musical understanding of the material used in combination with aesthetic ends that are in no way contained in the pre-existing musical material."[22] For precedent to be effective in any discipline, the sources must be transformed rather than transcribed. One term that accurately describes the use of precedent is attributed to the American literary critic Harold Bloom. In his book *The Anxiety of Influence*, he speaks of *misprision*, "a creative misreading that generates new knowledge."[23] It suggests an alternate conclusion to a predecessor's work, an imagining of what it could have been if it were taken in a different direction. While Bloom's idea was based on works of poetry, it can also be applied to architectural practice through the synthesis of multiple sources into a single project. Le Corbusier's Villa Savoye, for example, utilized qualities of ancient sources such as the precision of the Doric order and the geometry of Roman architecture instead of directly duplicating them. As Robert Venturi stated, "we look backward at history and tradition to go forward."[24]

It is not only architects' responsibility to be knowledgeable of the past, but they must also be prepared for new trends and ideas. The long lifespan of architectural projects means that they will need to be successful not only for the current social, economic, and environmental conditions, but also adapt to emerging situations. As Devon's studio professor noted, a library built today is different than one built fifty years ago. The advances in technology mean that they must now have computers available for research, and in the future might have even more technological adaptations. Architects must not only be knowledgeable about history, but must also keep up with current events to be able to accurately prepare for the future.

In a sense, the architect must act as a fortune-teller, reading the signs available to predict what will come to be. A *sign*, as defined by pragmatist philosopher and logician Charles Sanders Pierce, "stands to somebody for something in some respect or capacity."[25] Basically this means that objects can substitute for something else and in doing so they convey a message to the observer. In antiquity, the reading of signs was a ritual undertaken by seers to interpret nature. By reading the signs in the flights of birds, the entrails of animals, or the movement of smoke, it was believed that one could foresee future events. While these rituals are no longer considered credible, the underlying idea that "the spectator is supposed to see the representation of future events or distant scenes,"[26] can be easily applied to architecture. Again, we are reminded that Vitruvius suggested that architects read the climatic and environmental signs of the site to better understand what the future building would be, and even today, the concept of a building, based on reading the signs of the site, and social, political, and environmental trends, foretells the future building.

Perhaps the best way to consider the use of history in architectural practice is through Martin Heidegger's concept of *geschichte*, where history is neither fixed nor linear, and the past and future converge in the present.[27] When developing an architectural concept, you must not only draw from history and the precedents of previous designs, but must also have an understanding of what is likely to happen in the future, and design accordingly. Not only will this create the most viable and timeless building, but it will also make for a design that is dynamic, drawing on the past and the future. The multi-dimensional nature of architecture requires not only looking back and looking forward, but also looking horizontally, incorporating a broad range of subjects and influences into the development of a concept.

LOOKING HORIZONTALLY: AN ANALOGY

Jack was beginning his first day of school and was talking to his advisor about the courses he needed. Jack questioned why he needed such a range of courses such as English, philosophy, and physics if he wanted to be an architect. "Why shouldn't I just take studio? I just can't see why any of these other courses will help me become an architect," Jack said defiantly. The advisor, having heard all this before, smiled at Jack and pointed to a small reproduction of an Egyptian statue that was sitting on the shelf behind her desk. She said, "Jack do you know who that is?" Jack shook his head no. The advisor smiled and said, "That's Imhotep."

She pointed to a photograph of a building in Egypt, hanging on the wall behind her desk, and continued, "Imhotep was the designer of this pyramid and he became an example for future architects. He was Pharaoh Zoser's High Priest and the first recorded architect. In a culture such as Egypt's, the chief architect was at the top of the

2.6 A statue of Imhotep in the Louvre

governing hierarchy. Imhotep was revered for his great wisdom as a scribe, astronomer, magician, and healer. Architecture was simply one of the many fields of learning he commanded."[28]

The advisor leaned back in her chair and said, "Now I think it's interesting that Imhotep's broad background is not far removed from the education recommended centuries later by the Roman architect Vitruvius.[29] Did you know that Vitruvius' book on architecture was one of the primary books that influenced the Renaissance?" She went on, "It's Vitruvius' position on the education of architects that still influences us today. But let me start with why."

"First of all Jack, a man such as Vitruvius, like many in Rome's elite, was influenced by the Greeks. To the Romans, the Greek philosopher Plato would have been highly regarded. Unfortunately, architects and artists of his time did not impress Plato for he believed that they were simply uneducated craftsmen. To Plato, architects as well as other artists were mere makers of images, fabricators or manufacturers of shadows and illusions, purveyors of make-believe. Plato places them and their work in the lowest level of his divided line of knowledge.[30] To Plato poets and musicians were inspired, and inspiration is transmitted even to the bards who only recite the poet's songs, but sculptors and painters are seen as working solely according to the established rules of mechanics."[31]

Jack's advisor said, "You know Jack that artists and architects can persuade many people through their work. It seems likely that Plato felt that the craftsman architects were manufacturing disturbing, uninformed, and uneducated influences on Greek society through their designs. I think that Plato did not trust the ability of uneducated craftsman architects to create true thoughtful buildings. Instead, Plato offered the idea of a well-educated philosopher-king as a means of setting the standards for Greek society. What qualities are necessary for those who would be capable of developing the standards required to wisely pilot the ship of state? The answer Plato proposed is excellent discipline, a high level of education and talent. The high level of education seemed to be absent from the background of the Greek craftsman architects, who held such power to persuade."

"Vitruvius believed that architects must have a natural gift or a talent for architecture and a desire to learn. Certainly an architect has a great deal to learn about the profession, but beyond the craft of architecture, what should the student of this field know? The Greeks heavily influenced Roman architects, and we know that Vitruvius was aware of the writings of Plato, since he mentions him frequently in his *Ten Books of Architecture*. It is thus possible to make connections between the education of Plato's Guardians, the ruling class set forth in Book V of the *Republic*, and that recommended for the architect by Vitruvius. Plato believed his guardian class should be selected from those who show talent and sufficiently high intelligence. He wrote that they would, subsequently, be educated in order to gain knowledge of true being, from knowing the changing objects of the visible world to the eternal truth of the intelligible world."

"Vitruvius tried to balance theory and practice. He recognized that an architect with knowledge only of theory was half an architect. He probably was concerned that architects would be creating illusions of the truth; therefore, he recommended that architects should know philosophy as a means of explaining the true nature of things. In conclusion, Vitruvius wrote, 'But in respect to the meaning of my craft and the principles which it involves, I hope and undertake to expound them with assured authority, not only to persons engaged in building but also to the learned world.'[32] It can be inferred that Vitruvius was also reacting to a change in the architect's relationship with society. Certainly, Vitruvius recommended that architects have a solid background in the practice of architecture combined with an excellent general education. He believed the architect could produce successful interpretations and should present those interpretations through well-measured buildings."

"Certainly Jack," said the advisor, "this Roman view of the education of architects influenced the Renaissance view of the architect which remains today. Of course this view of architectural education continues for a reason. Ask yourself, can we ever work alone on an architecture project? Buildings are almost always too large and require other professionals. Architects must lead others in the role of master craftsman, and collaborate with and understand the workings of many other fields. You need to be able to speak the language of these many fields. It's a bit like becoming a conductor of an orchestra, understanding the abilities of the separate sections and instruments and coordinating all together. There is also the importance of understanding interdisciplinarity, since the inspiration for your designs are likely to also come from outside of architecture and design. You can get very interesting ideas about design from medicine, business, literature, science, or engineering. Look at the Beijing National Aquatics Center, for example. PTW Architects were inspired by the natural formations and structures of soap bubbles, and their research resulted in not only an interesting concept, but also a structural form based on natural geometry."

2.7 The night view of Beijing National Aquatics Center

Imagining

CONVERSING TO LEARN

On the third day of studio, the professor begins the class by saying "Continue to work on your projects, and I will come around and talk to you about your concepts and your reasoning." Amanda is nervous, she does not have an idea as to where she is going with the project yet and does not feel ready to talk about her design. Later that afternoon when Amanda's professor pulls up a stool at her desk Amanda sadly states that she has nothing to discuss, and perhaps the professor should move on to someone else. Her professor says that now is exactly the time to start talking, since even if Amanda doesn't have a concept yet, a discussion might help her thinking. What Amanda does not know, and will soon find out, is that dialogue and discourse can facilitate the early stages of design.

One technique, suggested by her professor, that may help Amanda to get started, would be to consider all possible alternatives. The term *brainstorming* was coined by Alex Osborn in the mid-1960s, as a way for corporations to find new ideas.[33] Basically, it is a method that uses free association, in a group setting, to explore thoughts never before considered. It is a process to suspend conscious intention to allow the formation of unconscious images.[34] Brainstorming involves a group of people who have defined an objective, then sit down to express any related ideas without restriction. Not unlike exploring various iterations, the process depends upon ignoring limits for a period of time. Brainstorming considers four principles: the focus is on the quantity of statements put forth, criticism is withheld until the process is completed, everyone in the group welcomes unusual approaches, and the intent is to combine and improve on what has been previously put forward.[35] Osborn believed that brainstorming sessions should have time limits, and end with analysis and agreed upon actions. Brainstorming can be effective because when anyone expresses an idea, it stimulates many more ideas in the minds of others, and forms a train of thought dependent upon association.

Psychologists view association as the ability to encourage the mind to see new possibilities by allowing one idea to inform another. This process is usually spontaneous and can provide new insight by stimulating suggestions. For architects and designers, the activity of association does not need to be in groups, nor in the case of psychologists, to find hidden behavioral issues, but can be both verbal and visual ways to bring ideas into the mind for consideration. Artists have long utilized the unguided trains of thought that open possibilities. Most young people recall lying in the grass and observing the patterns of clouds that may resemble common figures or forms. Although a cloud may not actually look like a giraffe, for example, it contains enough similarity to remind the observer of forms seen in the past. This visual reference may be found in just about anything, and often more in things that are abstract. Artists know that the mind continually attempts to find order in chaos, and thus it is always trying to relate what is seen to what one can comprehend. They understand the necessity to consider the unregulated impressions that may be stimulated by desire or need, before they are reined-in with practicality.[36] This is why, as mentioned previously, humans are intrigued by, and continually attempt to resolve, optical illusions or *trompe l'oeil*.[37] The philosopher John Locke, although suspicious of association, felt that it assisted humans to construct knowledge, and that knowledge could be found in comparing ideas and finding unique connections.[38] The ability to banter ideas back and forth to find inspiration can be visual or verbal, and although design students can sketch and build fast models for the development of initial concepts, verbal play can also be effective in locating beginnings.

2.8 Trompe l'oeil in Switzerland

What Amanda and her classmates may recognize, in more contemporary terms, is the concept of *free-play*[39] that can be compared to improvisation. The musician Stephen Nachmanovitch writes "Improvisation is also called extemporization, meaning both 'outside of time' and 'from the time.'"[40] He likens this improvisation to intuition that utilizes all our knowledge, our memories and everything we are. "Improvisation is intuition in action, a way to discover the muse and learn to respond to her call."[41] This free association of improvisation lets any thought follow another without criticism, encouraging unusual and interesting solutions.

Anything that is seen, heard, or experienced can be interpreted, and in contemporary society we are constantly inundated with images. Each of these images that stimulate us is open to being understood in relationship to our own experiences. Once that sign has been determined, the person who originated it no longer has control of its meaning.[42] In other words, a distance is formed, and people can interpret these messages any way they want.

Social critics, such as satirists and comedians, certainly use language and gestures to play with current events or media. They interchange and distort the messages from media. Since we do not always know what was originally meant by the message, humans can substitute and interchange the message and the messenger, and perhaps it is no longer important to recognize the origin.

As will be discussed more in chapter three, design has an infinite number of permutations and possibilities. It is important to be open to those possibilities, especially in the early stages of conception. The search may be the fun part, and sometimes the unknown (the aspects that lie in the realm of ambiguity) are the most attractive, as they contain the most hope and potential. The author Italo Calvino writes about his search for inspiration, "[m]y work as a writer has from the beginning aimed at tracing the lightning flashes of the mental circuits that capture and link points distant from each other in space and time."[43] To fully illustrate his imaginative and inspirational nature, we need to take a look at an excerpt from his book *Invisible Cities*, in which, Calvino writes:

someone puts his eye to a crack in a fence, he sees cranes pulling up other cranes, scaffolding that embraces other scaffolding, beams that prop up other beams. "What meaning does your construction have?" he asks. "What is the aim of a city under construction unless it is a city? Where is the plan you are following, the blueprint?" "We will show it to you as soon as the working day is over; we cannot interrupt our work now," they answer. Work stops at sunset. Darkness falls over the building site. The sky is filled with stars. "There is the blueprint," they say.[44]

In this way, Calvino is suggesting that authors (and designers) make unusual and unexpected links between items such as the stars and the ongoing construction of the city. Try a small test with yourself: envision what the city depicted above looks like and the symbolism behind what Calvino writes. Very much like successful comedians, whose weird connections are funny, this activity may discover unique and poignant places to begin.

Returning to likeness and the power of connections, literature, humor, and critique of contemporary culture makes use of verbal or written analogies and metaphors. Amanda may be reminded of her high school literature course where in a figure of speech a comparison can be made between two unlike things. But how can these word games help to locate architectural or design ideas? Metaphors can stem from sensory stimulation, thus for humans to engage imagination they must have many experiences to draw upon.[45] Philosophers from the last century have described pictorial metaphors that induce a train of understanding and meaning, but they can also make verbal connections. They write that ideas evoke ambiguous images or sensations that connect the pictorial with words, like poetic allusion.[46] Often word-play can spark interesting beginning points, such as literal or figurative expression – descriptions, tropes, or sensory terms.[47] An image can be conceived of as a picture, but can also be understood as a likeness. Especially in the use of memory and imagination, images have a similarity to things seen or experienced. Thus analogies and metaphors display various forms of likeness from the "very like" – facsimile, copy, clone, or replica – to the "less like" – such as a reference, allusion, or abstraction.

Alike things may be considered analogies, either the way they look or the ways that they function. The comparison of an analogy is not unlike association. In chapter one, Sandra was confused about how to find beginnings for her design, and she observed her classmates playing

2.9 Sydney Opera House at night from Harbour Bridge

word games, tearing cardboard, or watching the flutter of leaves. These are examples of how students can utilize analogies and metaphors to stimulate their imaginations either verbally or visually. Amanda's professor most likely would start a dialogue to suggest that she think of analogies or metaphors that involve the site, the client's needs, the context, or the goals for the project. As an example, a well-known building, the Sydney Opera House by the Danish architect Jørn Utzon has been the subject of speculation about its visual analogies or metaphors. Some have speculated that the large white precast panels that form the shape of the building resemble the sails of boats that may be appropriate for the site of the project

Imagining

in Sydney Harbour. In another example, the Spanish architect Santiago Calatrava, with training as a structural engineer, often begins design comparing the tensile characteristics of human or animal bodies as inspiration. He uses watercolor studies to morph bodies into sinuous structural components as visual diagrams that emphasize a comparison between the two.

Amanda's professor may inquire what she thinks are the priorities for the project, and thus begins a discourse that helps tease out an approach. After a period of time, the professor may call several students together to expand the discussion for more input. As a result of visual or verbal brainstorming and free association, Amanda and her classmates may derive some wild ideas stemming from the infinite number of combinations of site, context, or program. This brainstorming may get out of control and the ideas bantered around may seem almost ridiculous. The professor may then suggest ways that big ideas can be made to work. They are themes to start the process and need to be interesting enough to guide form and organization. Since small ideas will always be limited and can be easily compromised, it is much better to start with a big idea and then focus it. It is wise not to be too timid, remembering that strong ideas can be modified if necessary.

There is also great danger in using metaphors and analogies that are too literal. They can become similar to a one-liner joke that does not have depth and will not withstand the test of time. The first time they are comprehended they are interesting but can be perceived as tedious and shallow over the lifetime of a building. More sophisticated uses of analogies and metaphors are related to the users' experience in the building or the ergonomic shape of objects. A feeling of procession, for example, can be interpreted in many ways by different users, or even during each experience. The Museo del la Memoria de Andalucía in Granada, by Alberto Campo Baeza, exhibits a strong central circular ramp serving as the theme for the building. This strong concept is dominant in Baeza's initial sketches and is reminiscent of the courtyard of the Palace of Charles the fifth in Alhambra and the Reichtstag renovation by Richard Rogers in Berlin. Using a coliseum-like ability to view across a void, the space uses visual connection to accent human movement.

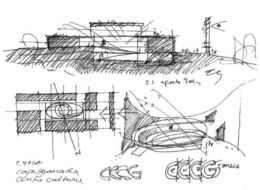

2.10 Andalucia's Museum of Memory sketch, Alberto Campo Baeza

As mentioned earlier in this chapter, it is nearly impossible to be totally original in the field of architecture. But, it is possible through dialogue and discourse to alter and distort precedent to a point where it becomes new. Not unlike paraphrasing, designers use reference to distort concepts and form in a method of exaggeration, deformation, or transformation. Artists use *pastiche* – fragments from or repetition of another artist's work or style – often to pay homage or to convey meaning. Caricature is similar in that it distorts or exaggerates the qualities of an original to find a truth beneath outward appearances.[48] Making a point by exposing a salient feature can certainly reference the characteristics of others' work. Caricature is often dependent upon humor or ridicule, and to poke holes in something certainly questions its presence and validity. Parody, although not necessarily dependent upon ridicule, can be seen as imitation, to mock, or comment on the work of others. The imitation usually requires a critical distance to create an ironic inversion or intertextuality.[49] For students of design or architecture this may mean exaggerating a prominent feature to emphasize the concept.

The studio settings of architectural or design schools ultimately present unique opportunities to experiment. Amanda and her classmates should not fear making mistakes and reworking. Often, it is the mistakes that result in the most interesting projects.[50] The ability to think without restraint or criticism is how brainstorming works and the early stages of design require this exchange of dialogue.

COMPLEXITY VS. SIMPLICITY

Coming up with a concept is perhaps one of the hardest parts of design work. The concept is the driving force behind all future design decisions, since it is the thesis or argument of the building. It determines the organization of spaces, materials, details, and overall atmosphere of the structure. The key to developing an effective concept is to ensure that it is full of possibility and sufficiently bold.

As discussed earlier, bold does not always mean that the concept must be overly complex. Although the term is often interpreted negatively, simple concepts are often the most effective. The philosopher John Locke defined a simple idea as one of uniform appearance or conception in the mind, something that cannot be created or destroyed, while a complex idea is constructed of a number of simple ideas.[51]

While simple can mean deficient in knowledge or insignificant, it can also mean pure, straightforward, unpretentious, and free from elaboration or artificiality.[52] It is sometimes the simplest of ideas that are the most clear and poignant. If a concept is so elaborate that it requires explanation, it needs to be edited down to be more coherent. A concept that is too simple, however, is equally detrimental. Too literal, and there is no room for possibility and interpretation.

Leila, for example, came up with an idea for a space that was based on the concept of rumination. On the one hand, rumination can mean the action of revolving something in one's mind, such as meditation or contemplation. On the other hand, it can also mean the chewing by an herbivorous animal of partially digested food from the rumen (one of a cow's seven stomachs). Leila utilized these multiple interpretations of rumination into both the atmosphere and organization of the space she planned to design. She created a building that was based on the idea of moving from one space to another, much like the multiple stomachs of a cow, taking a moment in each space to contemplate. Her concept was simple enough that it could be easily understood, but it was also complex enough that it could be integrated into her design in a number of different ways.

As mentioned previously, coming up with a concept is just the first part of the process, and good concepts can be found in many places, from the functional to the metaphorical. Leila has been discussing with her professor how to tell if her concept is a good one, and if it will lead to a beautiful project, but the professor interjects that it may be too early to tell. The subjective qualities of architectural design make knowing when a project is "good" very difficult because there are so many variables, and part of evaluation involves personal experience. You might consider an analogy about how to identify when your architectural design projects are "good." It is akin to planning a dinner party. You buy a piece of fish and wonder if it is fresh. You do not possess definitive criteria

Imagining

to evaluate its freshness, such as a chart to tell you the specific shade of green, the exact firmness of the flesh, or a scale to determine the aroma. Instead, taste and the ability to evaluate quality are acquired with experience. The many years of analyzing good architecture hone architects' critical ability to determine quality. This critical thinking means that architects and designers must learn to utilize evaluation criteria and also recognize the skills gained through experience. A logical explanation of the correctness of a solution is not always possible since design is rooted in a sensitivity based on substantial experience. The process of working through the design, the iterations and development through drawings and models will help solidify and evaluate whether a concept is "good." Architects and designers can locate "good" concepts in abstractions and also in very concrete ideas. Although this book will discuss the evaluation of the process in later chapters when talking about criticism, it may be worthwhile to explore the meaning of beauty to put some of this question in perspective.

Philosophers have long contemplated the meaning of beauty. From ancient Greece, Plato felt that things defined as beautiful consisted of balance and proportion. Socrates expanded on this, and expressed that things appropriate and well proportioned are satisfying. He also believed that objects are beautiful if made to fulfill their function, meaning that which is beautiful is beneficial.[53] The later Greek philosopher Plotinus suggested beauty could be found in the virtues such as righteousness, and also in the divine intellect and ideal form. He, not too different than Socrates, introduced that unity, harmony, and craftsmanship are critical in understanding beauty. A further element discussed by Plotinus, which reoccurs in the Renaissance with the author, artist, and architect

Leon Battista Alberti, is the belief that beauty stems from the sum of the parts to make a whole. Things that are concordant and congenial are also beautiful, and beauty is synonymous with good.[54] Equating beauty with the idea of "good" has been a common theme throughout history. St. Augustine agreed with the Greeks and wrote that beauty is "unity, number, equality, proportion and order."[55] Not surprisingly, since the Renaissance constitutes a philosophical reflection of rediscovered ancient Greek beliefs, Alberti viewed ideal beauty in proportion by stating that "I shall define Beauty to a Harmony of all the Parts, in whatsoever Subject it appears, fitted together with such

2.11 Design element illustrating a golden spiral

Proportion and Connection, that nothing could be added, diminished or altered, but for the Worse."[56] This belief held by architects and designers, that beauty lies in the whole, continues to contemporary thought.

The philosopher David Hume in his work *A Treatise of Human Nature* again iterated that beauty is order in the construction of parts, but also spoke about how it provides pleasure, although not everyone is moved in a similar ways. Hume brought forth the importance of taste or judgment in defining beauty just as today the critic, as a reflection of society's beliefs, has a role in deciding what is beautiful.[57] Contemporary aesthetic philosophers believe that art evokes emotion, and do not necessarily make the judgment that a work of art is beautiful, rather its beauty lies in its conveyance of expression or meaning. Thus, an idea of beauty is open to interpretation.

After some research, Leila is more confused. Beauty can be found in order, harmony, and proportion. It is related to a divine ideal, in the vastness of nature and the sublime, and also can be identified if the composition is considered whole. But mostly beauty can be defined in terms of judgment that is developed with experience and learned through establishing good taste. Returning to deciding on a good concept she asks, "So why do I need to be the one to pick the concept. Won't I always just be following the directions of my boss or won't the client just tell me what they want done?"

Clients may have desire for a building but rarely know how to implement the process – this is the job of an architect. In an architectural office you will typically make and implement solid decisions concerning the quality of your designs. A "good" concept reflects how you think critically and solve problems. While it is true that you will most likely begin in an office working on part of a larger design, you will not remain in this capacity and will move into a leadership position to direct an entire project. School will allow you to practice for this future of leadership by developing your ability to collaborate with others, see the whole picture and then produce it. There are always many parts that come together to bring a design to completion. To be able to do this requires leadership abilities and that is why most schools of architecture see themselves as educating leaders not just training technicians. Schools want their students to take responsibility, and as an architecture student you are a leader in training. As an architect you will be responsible for clearly defining what the concept should be, and although the discipline depends upon collaboration, you will be required to take responsibility for coordination and organization. To do this successfully you need to develop a way of critical thinking, solving problems not yet thought about, and, in a way, foretelling the future of the building. While this may sound interesting or even fun it also comes with responsibility, for in the end you are to blame for failures.

Leila's professor tells her to think of the concept for her building in relationship to the whole of the future project. The walls, roof, windows, and such parts all come together to create a building. But what is the main intention or purpose of the building? While the client may know that they would like a library, court house, office building, or the like they generally cannot define exactly what that should look like, which is why they engage a designer. It is your job, as a designer, to define that purpose by understanding how and why the parts that make up a building come together. Once a concept or purpose for the building is determined, the various parts begin to take shape to perform certain functions. The concept helps to determine all future design decisions. For example, the windows of a library should help with the reading and maintaining of the books or the walls of an art gallery should help with the display and protection of the works of art. Such parts coming together and working efficiently are what makes the building actually work. You need to be able to find the parts that make the building effectively perform its intended task. Ask the question, do the parts that I'm selecting for my building support my intent? In the end you need to be able to take these parts and use them to clarify your idea through a physical design. However, remember that during the design process your intent may shift and change. This happens as you learn more about the whole of your design through the development and selection of the parts.

Now that you feel more confident that you have used your imagination to decide upon an appropriate concept, it is time to start design development. A conceptual idea needs to be realized into physical form. This can only happen through the manipulation of various media in order for you to see and, subsequently, comprehend the future design.

Endnotes

1 Philip Johnson, interview by Rosamond Bernier, *Camera 3* (1076; CBS), television.

2 A. D. Fitten Brown, "Muses on Pindos," *Greece and Rome* 8, no. 1 (1961): 22–26.

3 *The Compact Edition of the Oxford English Dictionary* (Oxford: Oxford University Press, 1971), s.v. "creation."

4 *Oxford English Dictionary*, s.v. "inspire."

5 *Oxford English Dictionary*, s.v. "imagination."

6 Edward Casey, *Imagining: A Phenomenological Study* (Bloomington: Indiana University Press, 1976), 81.

7 Mary Warnock, *Imagination* (Berkeley: University of California Press, 1976), 33, and see David Hume, *A Treatise of Human Nature*, ed. L. A. Selby-Bigge (Oxford: Clarenden Press, 1978).

8 Casey, *Imagining*, 80.

9 Ibid., 66–68, 99–100.

10 Ibid., 87–97, 101–104.

11 Ibid., 106–117.

12 Arnold H. Modell, *Imagination and the Meaningful Brain* (Cambridge, MA: A Bradford Book, MIT Press, 2006), 91.

13 Ibid., 116.

14 Reference to the Student Performance Criteria in Conditions for Accreditation, see National Architectural Accrediting Board (NAAB) and Canadian Architectural Certification Board (CACB).

15 Robert Venturi and Denise Scott Brown, "A Significance for A&P Parking Lots or Learning from Las Vegas," in *Theorizing a New Agenda for Architecture*, ed. Kate Nesbit (Cambridge, MA: Princeton Architectural Press, 1996), 308.

16 Maurizio Sabini, "Wittgenstein's Ladder: The Non-Operational Value of History in Architecture," *Journal of Architectural Education* 64, no. 2 (2011): 46–58.

17 Ibid.

18 Roger H. Clark and Michael Pause, *Precedents in Architecture: Analytic Diagrams, Formative Ideas, and Partis*, 4th ed. (Hoboken: John Wiley & Sons, 2012), v.

19 Fred A. Bernstein, "Hi Gorgeous. Haven't I Seen You Somewhere?," *The New York Times*, August 28, 2005.

20 Ibid.

21 Geneviève Alain, Tore A. Nielsen, Russell Powell, and Don Kuiken, "Replication of the Day-residue and Dream-lag Effect," *20th Annual International Conference of the Association for the Study of Dreams*, Berkeley, California, July 2003.

22 Ana Miljacki, "From Model to Mashup: A Pedagogical Experiment in Thinking Historically About the Future," *Journal of Architectural Education* 64, no. 2 (2011): 9–24.

23 David Rifkind, "Misprision of Precedent: Design as Creative Misreading," *Journal of Architectural Education* 64, no. 2 (2011): 66–75.

24 Robert Venturi, Denise Scott Brown, and Steven Izenour, *Learning from Las Vegas: The Forgotten Symbolism of Architectural Form* (Cambridge, MA: MIT Press, 1977), 3.

25 See Daniel Chandler, *Semiotics: The Basics* (New York: Routledge, 2002).

26 Bronislaw Malinowski, *Magic, Science and Religion, and Other Essays* (London: Souvenir Press, 1974), 140.

27 Saundra Weddle and Marc Neveu, "Introduction: Beyond Precedent," *Journal of Architectural Education* 64, no. 2 (2011): 6–8.

28 See E. Baldwin Smith, *Egyptian Architecture as Cultural Expression* (New York: D. Appleton-Century Co., 1938), and Spiro Kostof, *The Architect* (New York: Oxford University Press, 1977).

29 Marcus Vitruvius Pollio, *De Architectura*, trans. Frank Granger (Cambridge, MA: Harvard University Press, 1985), 7–11.

30 Plato argues that there is only one form or idea of a couch. The craftsman initiates this idea making the couch of specific material while the painter produces only the optical appearances of the couch from a certain angle and is twice removed. See, *Plato: Apology, Crito, Phaedo, Symposium and Republic*, trans. B. Jowett (Walter J. Black, 1941).

31 Moshe Barasch, *Theories of Art, from Plato to Winckelmann* (New York: New York University Press, 1985), 23.

32 Vitruvius, *De Architectura*, 28.

33 See Alex Osborn, *Applied Imagination: Principles and Procedures of Creative Problem-Solving* (New York: Scribner, 1963).

34 Ibid.

35 Ibid.

36 Monroe Beardsley, *Aesthetics: From Classical Greece to the Present, a Short History* (Tuscaloosa: University of Alabama Press, 1985), 172.

37 *Trompe l'oeil* is from the French "to deceive the eye." It is manifest in art as an optical illusion of a three-dimensional scene.

38 Beardsley, *Aesthetics*, 174–175.

39 Stephen Nachmanovitch, *Free Play: Improvisation in Life and Art* (New York: Tarcher, 1991), 18.

40 Ibid.

41 Ibid., 41.

42 See Jacques Derrida, "Structure, Sign and Play in the Discourse of the Human Sciences," 1966, first a lecture and then published in the journal *Writing and Difference*.

43 Italo Calvino, *Six Memos for the Next Millennium* (Cambridge, MA: Harvard University Press, 1988), 48.

44 Italo Calvino, *Invisible Cities* (San Diego: Harcourt Brace Jovanovich, 1978), 48.

45 Modell, *Imagination and the Meaningful Brain*, 32.

46 W. J. T. Mitchell, *Iconology: Image, Text, Ideology* (Chicago: University of Chicago Press, 1987), 23.

47 Ibid., 24.

48 See Ernst Gombrich and Ernst Kris, *Caricature* (London: King Penguin Books, 1940).

49 See Linda Hutcheon, *A Theory of Parody: The Teachings of Twentieth-Century Art Forms* (Champaign: University of Illinois Press, 2000).

50 Stephen Nachmanovitch names this the power of mistakes.

51 See John Locke, *An Essay Concerning Human Understanding* (New York: Oxford University Press, 2008).

52 *Oxford English Dictionary*, s.v. "simple."

53 Beardsley, *Aesthetics*, 39–43.

54 Ibid., 80–83.

55 Ibid., 93.

56 Ibid., 125.

57 See David Hume, *A Treatise of Human Nature* (New York: Dover Publications, 2003).

Playing

Chapter 3

This is the real secret of life – to
be completely engaged with
what you are doing in the here
and now. And instead of calling it
work, realize it is play.

Alan Wilson Watts

Chapters one and two discussed ways to begin the design process and how to go about finding an appropriate concept. Chapter three now explores using media to help you develop your design using the ideas of play, rough drafts, and *festina lente*. This chapter also touches briefly on the advantages and disadvantages of utilizing specific media to help visualize your intentions. Although discussing design, the intent is not to explain precisely what you should design for a particular project, nor the moves you should make at each stage along the way. This chapter is also not concerned with how to

present a final product (as can be seen in the picture shown here) where the model is highly finished and appears to have been built for a different purpose than design

3.1 Kelley, Stone, and Kock view the model of Electronics Research Center

exploration. The three architects from the 1950s are presenting an after-the-fact model, one that is not about design development but solely for presentation in a professional setting, and this is not a type of model that you should build while in school. Rather, this chapter explores the early, often messy, explorations that are about thinking and discovering, and embraces the playful joys of creativity.

Alex, a beginning design student, and his classmates have received an assignment to design a small space for contemplation. The project description asks them to consider issues such as path and entrance, and present their projects three-dimensionally by building a physical model. Alex worked hard to formulate a concept, looking for inspiration and talking about it with other students, and then spent day and night building a detailed model. Unfortunately, when Alex presents the model in his first preliminary critique it does not receive a good reception or grade. His studio instructor tells him that she wants to see more of the process he used to get to his final design. Alex is confused, he spent hours creating a perfect model, and his instructor wants to see messy sketches.

What Alex does not realize is that a key goal of design studio is to get him and his classmates to develop a process to think and effectively work through various concepts. The instructor knows from experience that the first idea that comes to mind is rarely the best and it is through the process of studying your project that you can clearly view solutions. Instructors are reluctant to dictate a particular sequence of activities since they do not know what works best for each individual. Instead, most instructors will formulate a project statement that places you in an environment to experiment with different media such as a series of study models. Knowing that each student thinks differently, a beginning design instructor may remain purposefully vague to allow, or even force you to find your own design and avoid each student arriving at the same solution. It is in the studio environment that you can learn what medium and level of clarity is necessary for you to understand and present a clear solution to an architectural challenge.

As you have seen in earlier chapters, to design a specific response to an assignment, you first need to decide what you are attempting to accomplish. Likewise, you should now decide what questions about the project are most important to resolve. In other words ask yourself, what are the critical issues necessary to finding a thoughtful design solution, and how much time do I have? If, for example, you are designing a museum you may wish to focus on creating a relationship between places to observe

and learn, and places to store artifacts. You need to first decide what aspects are most important in a successful museum so that you can refer back to them as you progress and ask if they are working as intended.

All forms of media, as long as they are quick and can be easily manipulated, allow you to think more clearly about a project. There are several reasons for this: first, as stated in chapter two, it is very difficult to imagine something you have never seen

3.2 First year Architecture student with model

before, as new forms are typically combinations of things you have previously seen. With this said, you must build models, sketch, and construct digital representations to visualize the qualities and form of what you are designing. Another reason to manipulate materials stems from the fact that altering drawings, models, and images on the computer or by adjusting a piece of millboard is easier and less expensive than changing elements in the finished building. Thus, the substitute media allow you to alter your designs quickly and with considerably less investment.

With enough experience, you may learn to significantly imagine form in your mind and subsequently produce this form. The aesthetic theorist E. H. Gombrich calls this an act of matching what is in your mind's eye.[1] He suggests that we try to imitate what we imagine or what we see in our minds. We all know that it is very difficult to make something that matches perfectly with what we imagine because the forms in our imagination are vague, have undefined boundaries, or these forms escape easily when we try to replicate them. Gombrich also writes that when we make or draw something, we evaluate it against what we imagine. We craft the shape and then test whether it matches this ideal. We then alter the object or sketch until it comes close to our idea or it reaches a point where it is an acceptable form. He calls this *making and matching*. A process of design means that you must see something to evaluate whether it is a correct or acceptable solution. The Italian architect Carlo Scarpa expressed this concept well, writing, "I want to see things, that's all I really trust. I want to see, and that's why I draw. I can see an image only if I draw it."[2] This is thought provoking as it can begin an exploration of how drawing helps architects to "see" and understand. This is why you may be asked to sketch your visit to a site, as discussed earlier, rather than relying solely on photographs. Through the action of making something, or studying it enough to draw it, you are able to understand its function, materiality, interconnected parts, and form.

A design process is typically an attempt to define something. In Alex's case, he is being asked to move his designs from pure possibility – a stage where everything is possible and nothing has been ruled out – to a clearly defined and designed space.[3] Playing with media is helpful for creating definition and can be used throughout the design process, mediating between what Alex doesn't understand and his finished designs. Media such as models and sketches help him to make visible the invisible, offering an understandable way with which to develop and define the project.[4] Let us turn now to some of the basic things to consider when spending time visually articulating your ideas about design.

PLAYING

Jun is a first year student asked to design a monument to honor a famous person. He begins to sketch out an idea, but finds himself getting caught up with getting the sketches just right. During an initial desk critique, his instructor tells him to play with his design through rougher, freer, faster sketches to develop a stronger concept of the monument. Jun soon realizes that most of his professors feel while in school, design process is as important as the final product.

The ability to play with your ideas is a critical part of developing a design. Playing with a design allows you to clarify an idea or to try out a potential solution. It supports the ability to work out a solution to a problem and to learn without dangerous or expensive errors and their ramifications. Think about how children learn about the world through playing roles that prepare them for the future, such as playing house or constructing roads in a sandbox. When children learn from the action of representational play, the structuring role of play increases knowledge and influences comprehension. Architects also learn to play with their ideas through a variety of media such as sketches, drawings, or models. Play, in the context of the design process, can be an important part of learning about a future building.

To play successfully as a designer one needs rules or boundaries to test the work against.[5] These boundaries could include your general belief system (what you believe is right or wrong), the requirements of a given assignment, government regulations, or a philosophical position, to name a few. While these boundaries are of course always open to debate and should not be accepted without question, they remain extremely helpful in forming the rules that you can use to judge your work. Such rules act as a form of governor, working as a device to control something (in this case your design), and the output of that thing as compared to a standard. Governors prevent a machine from spinning out of control; however, an over-governed machine may become sluggish and run inefficiently. The philosopher James S. Hans writes:

> [play] requires that the "player" of the work of art accept the rules of the game that the work of art itself establishes – the player begins with his own fore-conceptions, but he must be led by the work itself, must accept the rules that work itself offers. Through the back-and-forth movement within the circle of the play, the rules become established [defined], the participant modifies his own projections accordingly, and he comes to understand the work of art precisely through the series of reversals of his own expectations which the correcting of his fore-projections involves.[6]

Comparing this idea of rules to that of a game, there always exists some adversary, some limitations of freedom, to overcome or to act against. It may be an opponent, a rule, chance, predictability, or a boundary of space, time, or physical being. Hans finds a similar connotation of boundaries or limits in the intention of play. As explained in chapter one, it might be desire that intensifies the search for an architectural solution. "Desire as I wish to consider it occurs as an aspect of the activity of play. If play is the activity, and production is the result of activity, desire is what provides the orientation and motivation for play."[7] You must actively want to find a solution to a problem, as it is the motivation that can ultimately drive a design. The rules for architects – of budget, site, or program – confine the play, and these limits structure their creativity; similarly, your design medium has boundaries in its form and the process has time limits. Your designs are also confined by your own skills, mindset, the program of the project, or the limits of your concept. These are the structuring aspects of rules that help the play to be productive. If a game is too restrictive, however, and the rules or boundaries are too rigid, it has no flexibility; consequently, the player may lose interest.

Play also adjusts to the game as it is played. For example, soccer players identify the strongest player on the opposing team, and modify their approach to compensate. They are, in fact, testing the tolerance, and generating new structures.[8] You will need to continually "react" to what you perceive in your design. This dialogue between architects and the materials they manipulate helps them adapt to changing situations.[9] This process helps you learn about the design and this dialogue assists you to understand what you are making.

What Jun and his classmates need to realize is that play is also representative, as it is the less serious situation that stands for another more serious action. The activity of play suggests *representation-of* [10] and *representation-for*,[11] where the choices provided to designers can either take on a pretender's role or play within the play to find meaning in the design.[12] Jun asks his professor how his design medium can represent. When Jun plays with his ideas, "representation-of," he is taking on a role where the action of the play presents him with new knowledge. Jun's professor states that sketches and models may describe the play employed to obtain an abstract idea rather than to represent a building. Also the materials he uses can act in a similar way to building materials, as they can stand in or be "representation-for" construction products. Although possibly not the same qualities (such as plaster is not identical to concrete) he can project onto these substitute materials to explore the substance through touch or its visual aspects. Manipulating representations of your design can be uncertain and make-believe, and can be not serious, but it can also be serious in its ability to assist in the activity of increasing understanding.

Returning to Hans, he feels that play requires both novelty and repetition so that the course of play incorporates the relationship between the two. "[P]lay shares one thing with games: a familiar structure that allows one to play with the unfamiliar."[13] In this case, the rules may be consistent but there is opportunity to be skilled or employ strategy. The difference adds to the knowledge and interest of the game, for if the soccer game was played exactly the same way each time, the same goals and the same passes, the winner would be obvious and all involved would quickly lose interest.[14]

The experiences of play may change our way of thinking. There remains a learning process involving interpretation that results in the production of play.[15] "The why of play is quite obvious: one seeks to play because one believes that the understanding achieved through play is more valuable than the kinds of understanding achieved in other ways."[16] Play helps to view issues in a new light, because the many opportunities to interpret give the play meaning where there is never a single understanding.

MAKING USE OF PLAY

Now that you have an understanding of play, how can you utilize this knowledge? Since you may be encouraged to quickly sketch potential designs, you should ask yourself which ones best explain the concept in your mind. If part of a sketch does not fit with the concept then perhaps you should eliminate that part. Your instructor may ask you to think of this as a type of game where you sketch and re-sketch to help clarify your design as a form of design editing. It is your responsibility to choose the rules of the game wisely. Some rules are more important than others, so think of what must be resolved immediately and what might wait for later. Returning to Jun's project, rules for the design of a monument to honor a famous person could include things that make you think about the person. For example, a famous peacemaker might suggest a monument representing peaceful concepts or a dictator might have some representation of total power. Then you can ask if your sketched designs are creating a peaceful atmosphere or totalitarian atmosphere as necessary. Sharp, threatening forms may work for the design of the dictator's monument but may not work for the peacemaker's monument, while a quiet pool surrounded by greenery and shade trees might. Remember that there is seldom a perfect answer to such a game, only more or less successful solutions.

When beginning to play with a design, you should quickly sketch an image of the main concept. If you are unsure of the concept, you may start with analogies or metaphors. Most importantly, you will need to put something on the paper to react to. Although putting down that first mark seems difficult as you may want to give it undue importance, it is better to draw anything – however unrelated – so that you are not intimidated by the blank sheet of paper. If, for your concept, you are trying to express a relationship of connection, you might want to sketch things that connect such as joints, hinges, or things that touch. Once you think you are close to a form, you may want to try to sketch the shape from many angles, and begin to alter its form in a process of making and matching. While you are doing this you can be thinking about the program, how the space will be used and the three-dimensional volume of the space. The boundaries of the program will assist you to focus the play and make decisions. Do not worry about how the sketches look, it is more important to create a dialogue with what you are drawing rather than be concerned with perfection. If you are self-conscious about your drawing skills, look at sketches by the influential and accomplished early Modernist French architect Le Corbusier. Although his sketches appear to be simple and crude, with shaky unconfident lines, they spoke to him and helped him visualize his thoughts. Remember, the relative beauty of the images is less important than how you interact with them. Let them direct your next steps and try to interpret what they are telling you about the project.

These sketches by the contemporary Spanish architect and engineer Santiago Calatrava illustrate aspects of play. Exploring the anthropomorphic qualities of a twisted rectangle Calatrava is utilizing the form of the human body as an analogy for the properties of structural elements. By comparing a building to a body, he is representing the concept of the forms and their functions through the sketches. Calatrava is learning about his design through visualizing his thoughts, finding knowledge in the activity of play, and is using the act of drawing to better understand his theme. The limits of the medium and the topic

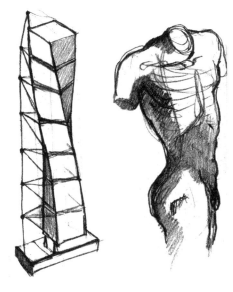

3.3 Sketch of human torso and building, Santiago Calatrava

that he proposed form boundaries around his thinking, and the focus of the progression of the design; the twist of each sketch and the juxtaposition between these images intensifies the comparisons.

A new project is assigned presenting many complex issues. Paige immediately goes to work, seemingly resolving her plan in a few hours, and spending the remainder of her time producing beautiful finished drawings. Hadi, on the other hand, begins sketching to work out the issues, but quickly discovers that it will take time to resolve all of them. Not wanting to lose his train of thought, he draws on a piece of tracing paper over the original image. In doing so, he finds that some of the line work carries through, and other lines change. This layering, the physical action of drawing in conjunction with critical analysis, leads to a scheme that has been iteratively optimized. When it comes time for an interim group critique, the professor quickly looks over Paige's elaborately rendered images. She questions a few things, before having a deep discussion on the iterations that Hadi developed. "But mine is so much more clear!" thinks Paige, not understanding that the most interesting part of her design can be revealed in how she developed it – a part she did not show or spend enough time on. Hadi's tracing paper drawings reveal his critical thinking and lead to a more robust discussion. As in the case of Alex, during early design phases the end product is not the most important part, and so although Paige's project was well represented for the early stages of design, it did not possess the same depth as Hadi's project.

In an effort to get you to play with your concepts, your studio professor may suggest that you come up with several alternatives to your current design. The reason for this

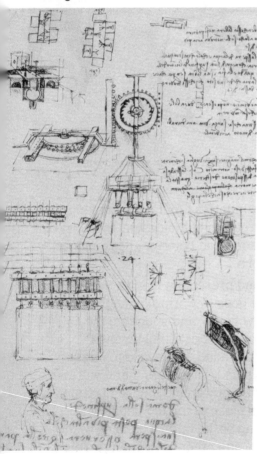

3.4 Sforza Monument, Leonardo da Vinci

is to help you see other possible solutions before settling on a design approach. Viewing alternatives may allow you to find a solution that you actually prefer, or may help you arrive at several directions that could be appropriate. These alternatives may assist you to locate various strong parts that could be recombined into a more logical or cohesive design. Now, it could be difficult to imagine other possibilities, so you might try a different concept, organizational strategy, or orientation on the site. Again, your professors know that the first idea is not necessarily the best idea, and through a process of trying alternatives you are able to question your solution. To help you understand the process of iterations, you may think of your design as a rough draft.

DEFINING ROUGH DRAFTS

A draft is a "preliminary version of a piece of writing or sketch,"[17] and can reveal ideas that flourish subconsciously, combined with those consciously conceived. Judith Robinson-Valery, professor of French studies within the realm of genetic criticism,[18] compares the rough draft to a diamond: "the more you polish a rough diamond, the more facets you reveal, that is reflecting surfaces creating ever-more complex interrelationships."[19] This analogy rings quite true in that the more iterations you make, the more opportunities and ideas a rough draft can reveal. Drafts can take the form of sketches, physical models, or three-dimensional computer models where each exists as a layer of the development of an idea over time. Much like tracing paper over a base drawing, bending or altering sketch models, or making digital three-dimensional iterations using "Save As" on the computer reveals a design's development and intention.

In literature, the draft or the marked-up manuscript has gained popularity over the last few decades. Literary critics became very interested in the preparing of a text and looked to authors' rough drafts for examples, naming this research genetic criticism. It was here that they discovered the plasticity and dynamism of the work, the split second encounters with an almost-character, a near-alternate ending, or the simple switch of one word to another. Ideas became layered upon one another, creating a literary palimpsest that traced the motion of the mind in the crossing out and additions.[20] It soon became obvious to these academics that rough drafts possessed something great that the final pieces of work did not: unobstructed freedom and the documentation of the changes involved in a thought process.

Similar to literature, architecture and design also have the ability to communicate ideas, and theorists have recently likened the structure of language to design. In some ways, language has rules and boundaries very similar to architecture, but the way each are interpreted reveals differences. For example, directions for assembly may be straightforward, while poetry encourages interpretation. In a similar way, architecture cannot be read for specific meaning. Using an example from architectural history, influential drawings, known as *paper architecture*, have been compared to preliminary drafts in literature, as have initial sketches, models, or notes on a design. Avant-garde architectural collaborators such as the German Expressionist architects Hermann Finsterlin and Bruno Taut in the 1900s, and Archigram, Superstudio, and Antfarm in the 1960s and 1970s created paper architecture as a mode of criticality towards the profession of architecture itself. These works of art, much like sketches and models, possess the same freedom unrestricted by any existing realities and the same boundless possibility.

In the Italian author and literary critic Italo Calvino's book *Six Memos for the Next Millennium*, he describes the draft in literature to be "a search for something hidden or merely potential or hypothetical, following its traces whenever they appear on the surface ... the word connect[ing] the visible traces with the invisible thing."[21] To Calvino, the draft is a world lost in an eternal search for answers to questions. In the process of this search, writers find themselves subconsciously documenting the world around them. Calvino, in describing multiplicity, notes that stories are "not just part of the 'color of the times,' but part of the work's very form, of its inner logic, of the author's anxiety to plumb the multiplicity of the writable within the briefness of life that consumes it."[22] Rough drafts, in any form, are thus reflections of ideas concerning particular ideals, styles, issues, and essentially the context within which they are created. In design, ambiguity is achieved through disregard for the typical limits of the world. The ambiguity of the draft, or of the drawing, breaks the status quo and initiates a paradigm shift. It is responsible for the beginning of a new method of thinking, of a leap from one system of thought to another and, ultimately, to gained knowledge. It is this ambiguity that ironically, while acting as an agent of change, gives definition.

Besides providing yourself time in your design process to utilize iterative solutions, you can also (early in the process) build-in the possibilities for change by allowing some ambiguity. If you build a model, complete a drawing, or allow a digital model to progress to a very complete product you are eliminating the ability to make quick changes – you begin to over-govern your design. The too complete model becomes so precious that you are afraid to alter it. If you see your design materials as a medium for the process then you can keep the design fluid – allowing the representations to encourage the alterations necessary for the rough draft. It is important to note, however, that efficiency must be employed when working within the boundless and free world of rough drafts. Decisions must be made in a timely manner, or your design may never reach a conclusion.

Contemporary architects use the iterations and ambiguity of rough drafts to explore the potentialities of their designs. Laura Tatum, architectural archivist, talks about the value of studying architects' rough drafts as "materials that tell the story of the design: early design drawings, architectural and structural drawings, early schematic drawings, different versions of a project presented to the client."[23] The projects are generational in the sense that they build upon each previous piece and this reveals a thinking process of making and matching that encourages architects to quickly make many versions that can be constantly adapted.

The Scandinavian firm BIG embraces rough drafts and the iterative design process. Many of their projects test multiple concepts before settling on a final design to ensure harmony with context and culture. Principle

3.5 Frank Gehry sketching on Plexiglass

3.6 Astana National Library concept diagrams, Bjarke Ingels Group (BIG)

architect and founder Bjarke Ingels stresses that "it is through improvisation and adaptation to unanticipated obstacles that we make our biggest breakthroughs," and "good ideas are sometimes resurrected from fossils of past evolutions,"[24] another reason to not only use rough drafts, but keep them for future reference and inspiration. The above image shows some of the many permutations developed for a specific site. Through many of these iterations you can see a play on similar forms, but all are still noticeably different from each other.

THINKING QUICKLY

Similar to Alex, Jun, and Paige, you will need to learn to swiftly investigate many ideas, including ideas developed out of rough drafts, and you should be able to use iterative thinking to make meaningful architectural designs. Paige can now enter the studio equipped with many model building materials confident she can engage in an interactive design process. She feels she has a foundation to begin but hopes her manipulations will help her make intelligent moves. The related topic of quickness will further elaborate ways to improve your design process.

Quickness is another concept examined by Italo Calvino[25] and it involves an economy of expression, thoughts about how time is relative, and swift reasoning and consciousness. The "relationship between physical speed and speed of the mind" can be seen when designers lose themselves in the act of play.[26] Quickness is also similar to play in the way it manipulates continuity and discontinuity in terms of time, through which it also can enhance learning through the acts of making things.[27]

The activity of quickness indicates life. The architectural theorist, Marco Frascari, describes a quickening as, traditionally, the first movement of a developing baby inside its mother; consequently, it is this movement that indicates life.[28] The quick sketch, gesture, or sketch model expresses life with active lines, and this fast image is not necessarily less informative than other types of sketches. Gesture drawing in fine art utilizes a fast sketch that does not outline a figure but rather renders its form or mass with line and shade. These and other types of sketches do not need to be a ponderously drawn-out image to be informativo and help you understand your design concept. Two or three-dimensional sketches are both economic and precise; they utilize minimal effort to show you something you did not previously imagine and something that is surprisingly true. Economy refers to using the minimum of anything that

can accomplish the purpose, and Calvino reinforces this by writing that folk tales are distinguished by structure, "economy, rhythm and hard logic."[29] In a story, the repetition of actions infused with different scenarios, reveals the play factor in learning.

The economy of lines, or expression, of a sketch discloses a quickness that is fast, intelligent, and witty. Here the relationship between physical speed and speed of the mind helps designers lose themselves

3.7 First year Ryerson University Architecture student sketching

Playing

in play. This out of body experience might be similar to a runner's endorphins. Once in the zone, your concentration eliminates other distractions. Designers and architects often become addicted to the act of designing, and certainly look forward to the intensity of their creativity. This time of concentration usually is manifest in dexterity of both the hands and the mind. Calvino, when writing about Galileo and his respect for quickness, writes that "[f]or him [Galileo], good thinking means quickness, agility in reasoning, economy in argument, but also the use of imaginative examples."[30]

HURRYING SLOWLY

Another concept, that helps illustrate the meaning of quickness, is *festina lente*.[31] Calvino took *festina lente* as his personal motto, which translated literally means to "hurry slowly." Hurry slowly, an apparent contradiction, reveals the opposite or mirror reflection that can induce a greater understanding. Viewing something from a different perspective helps you see new potential. If you view your sketch from the reverse side or turn your model upside down, you may find surprising insight. In a similar way, something can be both precise and imprecise at the same time, depending on how it is viewed. A Pointillist painting looks abstract and blurry when seen up close, but the picture can be recognized when seen from a distance. The dichotomous terms of *festina lente* make many new and fast mental connections, similar to how brainstorming often sparks architectural invention. How quickly an idea comes to you may require the precision and interpretation expressed in *festina lente*.

Calvino illustrates further with a Chinese story that is especially important to *festina lente* in the study of quickness.

Among Chuang-tzu's many skills, he was an expert draftsman. The king asked him to draw a crab. Chuang-tzu replied that he needed five years, a country house and twelve servants. Five years later the drawing was still not begun. "I need another five years," said Chuang-tzu. The king granted them. At the end of these ten years, Chuang-tsu took up his brush and, in an instant, with a single stroke, he drew a crab, the most perfect crab ever seen.[32]

Hurry slowly has meaning for the preparation of architects and designers and can help you learn to design. It would be incorrect to assume that this analogy advocates for the position that beautiful presentations and designs can be achieved on a moment's notice. Instead, the skills learned or perfected take time because the knowledge to draw something as simple as a crab can take years of observation, practice, and immense control of a pen or pencil. The beauty and truth found in simplicity emerges from experience. Quickness is about mental speed, and *festina lente*, as it contains the dichotomy of fast and slow, reveals how quickness can show intelligence. "A swift piece of reasoning is not necessarily better than a long-pondered one. Far from it. But it communicates something special that is derived simply from its very swiftness."[33] You will find, in your design process, that the repetition and refinement of forms and ideas will help work though architectural concepts, and that seldom does a successful solution arrive without thoughtful development and a lot of experience. To illustrate this idea, your professors may quote from the classical philosopher Socrates and say, "there is no solution; seek it lovingly."

Learning that comes from quickly playing with and developing design concepts can take place through the use of various media. Understanding the use of quickly formed models is important for design students because they assist the discovery and creative imagination that finds inspiration. In the same way, because of their complexity, models can take on a life of their own and inform architects and students of qualities never expected. A concept can present a precise idea but the model may not need to look precise. This dichotomy of precise and imprecise, can bring forth the intelligence of a conceptual metaphor built in three dimensions. In other words, you may need to design quick imprecise models that convey your ideas rather than wasting many hours building precise models before your concepts are worked out. This ability of models to work between and through media suggests that they can help you to clarify your ideas and shows how a quick model can cross between concepts.

Likewise, beginning with a quick and ambiguous sketch starts a process of abstraction that produces unexpected forms. These undefined forms can encourage manipulation and transformation. This progression offers designers the ability to edit and evaluate at various stages throughout the process. As an example of play, this manipulation encourages the repeatability and ritual of play where you are able to maintain the original and yet still experiment.

Since wit certainly means intelligence and humor that stems from making unusual connections – how can Paige employ wit and intelligence into her project, especially in light of *festina lente*? By quickly altering her various media, she can practice finding the relationships between ideas and form. She might also begin by considering the boundaries of the project to brainstorm possible alternatives. For example, it is easier to design on a restrictive site – one that is very narrow or steep – than an expansive plane. The reason for this is that the boundaries help you find ideas. On a steep site you may be required to try some alternatives such as cantilevers, placing the project on stilts, or excavating into the side of the slope. Those creative solutions come about from assessing the situation of the context – the boundaries. In the case of a large flat plane, there is little context to react to. The quickness of exploring unusual and seemingly edgy ideas will insert wit into the process. When you attempt unusual solutions, however, they require extensive care in making sure they can really work. The cantilever, for example, would mean tremendous effort and time to resolve the structural issues. So again, design requires consideration of many factors that need to work together: function, aesthetics, and thoughtful reasoning to ensure soundness.

USING MEDIA

What tools and techniques will help you develop a process that utilizes rough drafts, play, and quickness? For the next project, Valerie is assigned the task of designing and building a chair out of cardboard. This project involves the action of sitting, construction, and representation. A chair is a typical design project in architecture and design

3.8 Sketch models for a theater complex

schools because it is a full-scale object that can be built and then immediately tested for structural stability and comfort in relationship to its aesthetic qualities. But how should Valerie begin? First, she must evaluate how each medium would help her to develop her ideas for this particular project.

Building models is a great way to spend time with your ideas. Generally a model is a small object that represents another, often larger, object. Certainly a model can also offer a tentative description of a theory or system that accounts for all its known properties. For architects, landscape designers, and industrial designers, models are typically three-dimensional representations usually created in a small scale of a projected or existing structure showing how its components and proportions work together. The *Oxford English Dictionary* tells us that the word *model* originates from the vulgar Latin *modellus*. *Modellus* is a diminutive of the Latin *modulus*, a further diminutive of *modus*, which means to measure.[34] A model can be a preliminary pattern, serving as a plan, from which an item not yet constructed will be produced.

Architectural scale models can be an important part of the design process, but just how are they useful? First we might consider several important concepts about scale. To many, scale simply means a system of ordered marks arranged at fixed intervals that are used as a standard of reference in measurement.[35] Scale allows architects a means for climbing towards a definition, developing a balance or medium between a known and an unknown, creating a standard with which to refer and a way of peeling away to reveal that which is unseen. Models can help eliminate problems in perceiving a future building or product[36] and are useful in allowing architects and designers to perceive their developing concepts more clearly, and indeed spatially, making them less ambiguous than drawings. Models are used to view shadows, massing of forms, complicated intersections, and a variety of other issues concerning the design of future buildings or products. Models are used to visualize elaborate shapes and new design forms, allowing difficult spatial problems to be more thoroughly and effectively studied three-dimensionally. Working three-dimensionally allows for the discovery of conflicts before the construction phase, allowing us to solve these design problems before it is too late. We might say that a scale model is an important part of the process necessary for creating a clear definition and for demonstrating a proposed building or product.

There are several general subcategories of scale models used by architects when designing buildings. Sketch models are typically used early in the development of a design concept and are fluid and changeable in nature. They concentrate on the basics of space-refining elements and usually remain free from the attention to surface detail. Study models contain more detail and are more time consuming to build than sketch models. They are easily changeable and are used to study the site, a specific detail, or the overall building concept. Finally, presentation models are highly detailed, difficult to change and often expensive to build. You certainly have seen the perfect and seductive models of complete buildings, usually viewed under Plexiglass cases sitting in museums or lobbies of corporations. They are not models to be quickly changed or manipulated but present already completed ideas about the building's design. These are not the type of model we would like to talk about. Instead we will talk about the types of models most used in the design process: the sketch and study model. To understand how we can successfully use this type of model, let us consider what their purpose is in the process.

Many consider architectural models to be the most easily understood presentation technique. Even though architects are typically experienced in spatial thinking, their clients are generally not. Models are helpful in allowing clients to more clearly perceive a potential design. They can directly communicate ideas to the average person without the necessity of explaining complicated and confusing technical drawings. They take the place of words and may present a design more effectively than pictures. It may be cliché to state that a picture is worth a thousand words but it could be argued that a model can be worth at least a thousand pictures.

Architectural scale models are typically used as thinking mechanisms for defining, and these models differ from instruments such as transits, yardsticks, or measuring cups whose specific measurements are already well defined. This is because architectural scale models are created not only as a means of designing our life-sustaining buildings, but also partake in defining a society. This of course is not an easy task but one that typically fascinates architects.

Architectural models help define the architecture in its attempt at measuring what many consider God's work: the material world and its phenomena, or what we call nature. English architect and architectural historian W. R. Lethaby writes in *Architecture, Mysticism and Myth*, "Architecture, then, interpenetrates building, not for satisfaction of the simple needs of the body, but the complex ones of the intellect."[37] This situation occurs because, as Lethaby continues, "all architecture, temple, tomb or palace was sacred in the early days and is, thus, inextricably bound up with a people's thoughts about God and the universe."[38] Of course, thoughts such as this and how they are defined can be subject to interpretation and change. This is why specific scale models from different historical periods may physically appear quite similar, but there can be major differences as to what these models were seen as defining.

An architectural scale model is a useful mechanism for the demonstration of your designs. Of the multiple definitions associated with the word *model*, the French word *maquette* is probably closest to this concept. The key to the significance of a maquette is the concept of demonstration, a word that comes from the Latin *monstrum*, and means "to divine, portend or warn."[39] A demonstration offers a foreshadowing of coming events and allows a certain prophetic indication of meaning through marvel, prodigy, and wonder, and thus is closely related to the divine. Divine is directly related to the concept of God or perfection, and can also mean to foretell through inspiration, intuition, or reflection on the shape of future events.[40] The maquette allows architects to predict the future by interpreting signs and omens and can warn them of future problems while allowing wonder and surprise into the design process. A completed building also can serve as a kind of maquette to demonstrate transcendent concepts. It is possible to understand how various early monuments, tombs, and temples all operated as forms of architectural scale models during their times. Therefore, what remains of these past implementations of design helps define humanity's search to understand the perceived chaos of nature.

In Sydney Pollack's film *Sketches of Frank Gehry* (2006), the architect can be seen sitting with design partner Craig Webb in front of a cardstock sketch model of a building. They discuss it, and Frank Gehry says: "lets look at it for a while, be irritated by it, and then we'll figure out what to do." Gehry points to parts that he doesn't like, and they begin to cut out chunks of the walls and bend down the roof to meet the new walls, at which point he says it needs to be "crankier," crumpling a piece of paper to act as the new wall. The model, which at the start of the segment looked somewhat refined, is now hastily taped together with new components, continuously changing. This iterative play with the sketch model continues until he excitedly states "that is so stupid looking it's great!"

Returning to Valerie designing a chair, she decides that creating a series of sketch models may be a great start to develop her design. She immediately gets cardboard, and begins to cut and fold the material, allowing her to understand it through manipulation. In this case, the sketch model is made of the same material as the final product, so it is a useful place to start. But jumping into material testing will not alone make a functioning chair, so she moves into sketching.

As mentioned earlier, a sketch is a brief description or outline, "to give the essential facts or points ... without going into details."[41] Architects and theorists, writing about art and basic design, stress that drawing involves line. At the most basic level, a line is "a mark made by a pointed tool."[42] Drawing involves making marks that are initiated by the movement and force of your hand. In reverse, your eyes follow a line, and with that action the "line's potential to suggest motion is basic."[43] A line or mark made with the bodily action of hands has the ability to cause a reverse action as it attracts your eyes to follow it. This action spurs associative thoughts, as your mind sees something and then associates other thoughts.[44] The artist or architect perceives a line and responds with another. As discussed earlier in Aristotle's writing, James J. Gibson, psychologist and philosopher, believed it is reasonable to suppose that humans can think in terms of drawings.[45] Conversely, but consistent with his theories of visual perception, there cannot be vision without the cognitive action of thought.

Gibson writes about human contact with a drawing: "the movement of the tool over the surface is both felt and seen."[46] The gesture of this intimate participation with a sketch gives it meaning and individuality. The control of hand on drawing tool yields not a consistent line but one that is varied, thick or thin. Architect's sketches help them discover a concept at the beginning of a project, but can be used in all stages of the design process

3.9 Bay Adelaide North Tower sketch

and even as an observational recording long after the building is constructed. They may or may not be quick in terms of time, and they may have varying degrees of detail. Sketches may facilitate discovery and the first inspirations for conceptual beginnings, they can be part of the communication between parties involved in the process, or they are often a means to record mental impressions. Sketches can be employed to evaluate decisions and suggest refinement, they are used as diagrams to analyze a difficult thought, and they help designers to visualize and thus understand complex configurations. They can also assist to work through the mechanics of a detail. Sketches can assist comprehension, as philosopher Maurice Merleau-Ponty expresses when discussing the artists Klee and Matisse: "the line no longer imitates the visible; it 'renders visible'; it is the blueprint of a genesis of things."[47] "Rendering visible" implies an understanding deeper than an illusion. This may be a distinct feature of sketches, which are often incomplete and vague. Again, this is reminiscent of the sketch's role in seeing as understanding. The designer's mind must be able to immerse itself in the making.[48]

As a definition of sketches implies, they are often imprecise, lose their value as the design progresses, and are seen as a means to find something or communicate rather than as prized objects in and of themselves. They are usually, but not necessarily, loose, and lacking in detail.

Sketches are blinks of the eye, snapshots of the creative process. They are resting points for the wandering intellect on the quest for form – needed for keeping track and for checking; for being able to go back and find a new linear approach to an entangled train of thought, or even to take up an altogether difference course.

Sketches are catalysts for the mind and, at the same time, the basis for return.

Sketches are, to all intents and purposes, the medium of change. They represent a manifestation of the various stages of the process of "taking shape," of the quest for the ultimate form.[49]

Design sketches spark architects' and designers' minds to produce mental impressions and may be a visual assistance to brainstorming. As discussed in chapter two, their imaginations are open to many possibilities, since in a beginning stage no potentiality is ruled out. These options might be fragmented and vague, but they originate a thinking process. The architectural theorist Werner Oechslin feels that "the sketch is ideally suited

3.10 Digital sketch image

Playing

for capturing the fleetingness of an idea."[50] This quote emphasizes the intangible qualities of a sketch. Sketches are able to, in their relative imprecision, essentially move as fast as the hand moves, and as fast as the designer's mind. They are able to encapsulate a thought before it is lost.

After creating and playing with her sketch models, Valerie decides to sit upon her own chair in studio to sketch and begins to reflect upon the action of sitting, the motion and balance of the act. On layers of tracing paper, she begins to sketch the movement of a person sitting, and her concept begins to reveal itself. Working quickly, she sketches out an idea of what the chair could be, and then quickly transitions back to building from cardboard, testing her drawn ideas in three dimensions, and testing her concept in a physical form. As each method of exploration has its own advantages, it is valuable to move between them in order to see what can be learned from them. As Valerie continues to experiment with the material, she realizes that it is taking quite a while to build each of the sketch models, and so she opens her computer.

Although digital models are a valuable tool in the design process, in contrast to physical methods, they are removed from the constraints of the physical. It is interesting that the word *digital* derives from the Latin *digitalis*, "pertaining to fingers,"[51] suggesting a hand-made product, yet in the digital realm, fingers simply control the input of the information creating the model.

Because the digital model lacks physicality, it is limited by current hardware and software requirements. A digital model can be built to a scale, or can be scale-less and can be used to explore concepts quickly and imperfectly. An advantage to working in the scale-less realm of the digital is that all scales can be worked with; from the overall concept level, to the massing, down to details at later points in the project. Yet, here lies one of the inherent weaknesses of this working method: it is easy to get carried away and develop the project too quickly, move from concept into the finer grain, and get too detailed at an early stage. The project may have qualities of being both precise and imprecise. It is precise in that the inputted data have distinct qualities but imprecise because of the computer's abstraction. Since the digital realm places few limitations on what can be envisioned, it can be dangerous to build the project entirely in digital space. You may also realize that the precise qualities of images created digitally do not encourage changes.

It is, however, easy enough to avoid this. The Save-As function, though seemingly mundane, allows for exploration through iterative design. The computer's capacity for extensive data storage eliminates the preciousness of the model; the time invested is not lost if a wrong move is made, but rather the model can be built upon. Much as a rough draft would, using Save-As allows for a model to be built, added on to, have parts deleted, and then return to the original in order to quickly create another iteration. Working with digital modeling tools also allows for the quick translation of a sketch into a basic spatial premise, which aids in both the development and your own understanding of the project.

Unlike the manipulation of physical models, in digital space the constructs are based on the mathematical concepts of points, lines, planes, and their various combinations. Three-dimensional digital modeling tools are inherently based on physical processes; the commands are intuitively related to the real world. For example, within many digital drawing programs, there are commands such as *trim* that help us understand how something is being built, so that although we are working in the digital realm, we can imagine how we could make such a sketch model in the physical realm. However, outside of these physically rooted processes are the creative concepts which are much more difficult to perform in physical space. Commands such as *stretch*, *extend*, and *contour* allow for creativity, but should be tempered with a concern for how they can translate to physical form. An advantage of digital modeling, at later stages in the design process, is that it can also be used to generate information for physical sketch models, through fabrication strategies such as 3D printing, or laser cutting.

The architectural educator Branko Kolarevic argues that the information that we generate in digital modeling makes us akin to the master builders of the past. Using the computer to design allows for the quick translation of the design into scale sketch models or full-scale manufactured objects through digital fabrication technologies.[52] One of the main advantages of digital modeling is the information inherent to the model that the designer would not otherwise easily possess. Frank Gehry's office – one of the innovators in digital design – uses aerospace software called CATIA that allows for the creation of the project at a full scale in the digital realm. In *Architecture in the Digital Age: Design and Manufacturing*, Kolarevic gives the example of Gehry's pavilion at the Peix Hotel d'Arts on the Barcelona waterfront. The process began with a physical sketch model, which was translated into a digital surface model. As the formal qualities became digital, parts were able to be refined and further developed.[53] The wireframe, a representation of the surface through lines connecting vertices on the surface, was extracted, and used to develop the structure that would support it. From this development, the information generated within the model was used to create a physical scale model to test the process. From this, further tweaks could be implemented on the digital model; if it was not found to be satisfactory, this iterative play continued until the desired outcome was reached. The information found within the digital model was used to fabricate and construct the pavilion itself. It is important to note, much as in the case above, that this computation does not replace hand sketching and modeling, or other tools, but complements them. This is because within the digital realm the project loses the inherent advantages of physicality and depth. Thus, a project cannot be fully developed within the computer.

Valerie, now working on the computer, builds her initial digital model according to one of the cardboard sketch models she has built, and immediately saves. Then she creates a copy, and begins to edit, deleting and adding to it. Not happy with the result, she reopens the original file and begins to work on it. She prints out the line work, cuts out the pieces, and assembles a sketch model. This process of working between media continues until she has developed a design for a chair that she is happy with – one that has been conceptually and functionally developed through iterative play.

After having built a concept, spending time with your ideas is an important step in the development of a design. The ability to quickly play with your ideas is a critical tool that allows you to clarify ideas or to try out potential solutions. It supports the ability to work out a solution to a problem and to learn without dangerous or expensive errors. Swiftly investigating many ideas, developed out of rough drafts, models, sketches, or on the computer, will enable you to iteratively discover your design through playing with the ideas out of which it is born. This allows you to use conceptual thinking to make meaningful architectural designs. It is very important to note that there must be a balance between time spent with your idea, and the time spent representing your idea. Often students equate spending time with taking up a lot of their time, but these two do not equate. Having spent hours on a design, but not really working through it, students may be perplexed by their unexpectedly low mark. Spending time also implies being effective with time, and allowing the design to evolve, rather than designing hastily and then spending time making the drawings perfect, or making an incredibly detailed model.

But how can you ensure that you are spending your time effectively? Because the design process is non-linear, the way time is spent on a project is almost never the same from project to project or from person to person. Everyone has his or her own way of working, and it will be useful to find what methods work for you. All forms of media, as long as they can be manipulated and let you play with them, will allow you to think more clearly about a project. Where some designers and architects jump between all the media mentioned, some may use only a few, and the time spent with each will likely not always be equal. You will find, as your own design process develops, that the repetition and refinement of forms and ideas, through play, will help work though architectural concepts, and that seldom does a successful solution arrive without thoughtful development and a lot of experience. This thinking and doing are inherently interconnected, creating a feedback loop. So where do you stop? When has the idea evolved enough to begin editing? There is no true answer to this question. The nature of the design process is one of intuition and experience; and at some point you will likely know when you are ready to move to the next step.

Endnotes

1 See Ernst H. Gombrich, *Art and Illusion* (Princeton: Princeton University Press, 1984).

2 Francesco Dal Co and Giuseppe Mazzariol, *Carlo Scarpa, The Complete Works* (New York: Electa/Rizzoli, 1984), 242.

3 See Edward S. Casey, *Imagining: A Phenomenological Study* (Bloomington: Indiana University Press, 1976).

4 Merleau-Ponty connects concepts of the visible and invisible to the imagination and the senses of the body.[a] He tells us that the invisible can be imagined but cannot be seen. He writes, "Meaning is invisible, but the invisible is not the contradictory of the visible: the visible itself has an invisible inner framework and in in-visible is the secret counterpart of the visible."[b] Merleau-Ponty believed the invisible is not non-existent but that it pre-exists in the visible. He writes, "This visible not actually seen is not the Sartrean imaginary: presence to the absent or of the absent. It is a presence of the imminent, the latent, or the hidden."[c]

a Maurice Merleau-Ponty, *The Primacy of Perception*, trans. James Edie (Evanston: Northwestern University Press, 1964), 162–164.
b Maurice Merleau-Ponty, *The Visible and the Invisible*, trans. Alphonso Lingis (Evanston: Northwestern University Press, 1969), 215.
c Ibid., 245.

The basics of this process of definition are useful for fields outside of design as well. For example, the American philosopher, John W. Miller writes, "by what method therefore can the study of philosophy proceed? ... Only through the definition of the term." Since the roots of the term come from the Latin *definire*, meaning the setting of bounds or limits, the study of philosophy seems quite similar to the process of design. But what do we mean by definition? The *Oxford English Dictionary* writes that the etymology of the word *definition* comes from the Latin word *definire*, which means "the setting of bounds or limits." To define something is to create boundaries in order to designate its exact meaning. It is interesting to note that the word *designate* is closely related to the word *design*, which means "to mark out."

5 Philosophers who write about play agree that there are several aspects that identify play: it has boundaries and limits, it is representative, it enhances learning, it involves, and it has a structure of repeatability.

6 James S. Hans, "Hermeneutics, Play and Deconstruction," *Philosophy Today* 24, no. 4 (1980), 306.

7 James S. Hans, *The Play of the World* (Amherst: The University of Massachusetts Press, 1981), 51.

8 Ibid.

9 See Johan Huizinga, *Homo Ludens: A Study of the Play Element in Culture* (Boston: Beacon Press, 1955).

10 See Joel C. Weinsheimer, *Gadamer's Hermeneutics: A Reading of 'Truth and Method'* (New Haven: Yale University Press, 1985).

11 See Richard Wollheim, *Art and Its Objects* (New York: Harper and Row, 1971).

12 See Gregory Bateson, *Steps to an Ecology of Mind* (London: Jason Aronson, 1972).

13 Hans, *The Play of the World*, 28.

14 Ibid.

15 Ibid.

16 Ibid., 11–12.

17 The *Compact Edition of the Oxford English Dictionary* (Oxford: Oxford University Press, 1971), s.v. "draft."

18 The area of genetic criticism (*critique genetique*) began in France as a rather new field of research based somewhat upon the ideals developed out of the French Structuralist movement

in the 1960s and 1970s. By examining physical documents such as drafts, author notes, and previous manuscripts, genetic criticism is primarily concerned with aiming to "restore a temporal dimension to the study of literature … [that] is mainly concerned with how texts are produced." In other words, genetic criticism could very well be defined as the study of "textual invention." With an interest in the sociological and psychoanalytic aspects of a written work, genetic criticism focuses on the more abstract notion of the movement of writing through its earlier documents. It essentially aims to reconstruct the writing process by looking at the events evident in the draft work itself. Although drafts had been a long known point of interest, this field of critical research only gained true momentum when the novelist Edgar Allen Poe published *The Philosophy of Composition* in 1846. With this work, Poe argued that the drafts and manuscripts of great works be studied as intently as their finished counterparts. He called for an author to "detail, step by step, the processes by which any one of his compositions attained its ultimate point of completion." Authors inspired by such work, including Stephane Mallarme and Paul Valery, became true proponents of genetic criticism with their continual writings asking for a shift of focus from product to process. Louis Hay, who was studying manuscripts at the Bibliotheque Nationale, proposed that "the creative process is itself a worthwhile object for literary studies" and that a new perspective on the critical analysis of literature would be gained by studying the manuscripts of authors. In all, genetic criticism has inspired other creative fields, including design, to look deeper than the finished

product. It is for this reason that rough drafts, through sketches or models, are an essential element in the development of an idea, and the design process itself. See Jed Deppman, Daniel Ferrer, and Michael Groden, *Genetic Criticism: Texts and Avant-textes* (Philadelphia: University of Pennsylvania Press, 2004).

19 Judith Robinson-Valery, "The Rough and the Polished," *Yale French Studies* 89 (1996), 60.

20 Italo Calvino, *Six Memos for the Next Millennium* (Cambridge, MA: Harvard University Press, 1988), 48.

21 Ibid., 77.

22 Ibid., 112.

23 Quoted in Mark Alden Branch, "The Architect at Work; Art history isn't just the finished product. You also need to see the rough drafts," *Yale Alumni Magazine* (2011).

24 Bjarke Ingels, *Yes Is More* (Copenhagen: Evergreen, 2009), 23.

25 Calvino, *Six Memos for the Next Millennium.*

26 Primary aspects of play include: play as a way to gain knowledge; play as repeatable – infusing the different into ritual; play is only play during the action of play; play acts as a representation- for another action; play requires boundaries; and play is distinctive in the ability to lose oneself in the activity of play. See Hans, *The Play of the World*, Bateson, *Steps to an Ecology of Mind*, Hans-Georg Gadamer, *Truth and Method* (New York: Academic Press, 1977), Johan Huizinga, *Homo Ludens; A Study of the Play Element in Culture* (Boston: Beacon Press, 1955), and Roger Caillois, *Man, Play and Games* (New York: The Free Press, 1961).

27 This activity can be a form of give-and-take that implies an action and a response, distinctive of play.

28 From a seminar by Dr. Marco Frascari at Georgia Tech, 1989. Also consider the concept of body memory in writings by

Edward Casey, as being "intrinsic to the body, its own ways of remembering: how we remember in and by and through the body." Edward Casey *Remembering: A Phenomenological Study* (Bloomington: Indiana University Press, 1987), 147. Body memory is similar to Merleau-Ponty's theory of the body as habitual. Maurice Merleau-Ponty, *Phenomenology of Perception*, trans. Colin Smith, (New Jersey: The Humanities Press, 1962), 142–147.

29 Calvino, *Six Memos for the Next Millennium*, 35.

30 Ibid., 43.

31 *Festina lente*, "make haste slowly," was first referenced in the big Aldine edition of Erasmus' works in 1508. He writes "no other proverb is as worthy as this one." Erasmus cites an expression from Aristophanes, "make haste hastily," and it was altered later. Octavius Caesar is known to have used the phrase repeatedly. Emperor Titus had a coin stamped bearing a dolphin and an anchor, which could illustrate this dichotomy. Erasmus offers three overlapping interpretations of this royal adage: first, "it would be better to wait a little before tackling a matter; when a decision has been reached, then swift action can be taken"; second, "the passions of the mind should be reined in by reason"; third, "precipitate action should be avoided in everything." *Mimesis: From Mirror to Method*, eds. John D. Lyons and Stephen G. Nichols, Jr. (Hanover and London: University Press of New England, 1982), and Thomas M. Greene, "Erasmus's 'Festina Lente': Vulnerabilities of the Humanist Text," in *The Vulnerable Text: Essays on Renaissance Literature* (New York: Columbia University Press, 1986), 132–148.

32 See Calvino, *Six Memos for the Next Millennium*. Ernst Kris and Otto Kurz tell a similar story in their book *Legend, Myth, and Magic in the Image of the Artist* (New Haven and London: Yale University Press, 1979). They use this story to emphasize the position of the artist as having divine talents not understandable to laymen.

33 Calvino, *Six Memos for the Next Millennium*, 45.

34 *Oxford English Dictionary*, s.v. "model."

35 Other definitions of scale can offer interesting and unusual insight into a deeper meaning of the term. The word *scale* derives from the Latin *scalae*, which means ladder, and currently scale can mean to climb. A scale can be a mechanism that provides an understandable balance between a known and an unknown. When a fisherman scales a fish he or she, through the act of peeling away, reveals something which was previously unseen underneath. A standard of reference or reference standard is a term borrowed from the field of measuring and simply means to direct to the established fixed rules. In measuring, an unknown is measured by comparing it with a known thing that has been previously developed. Such reference standards are calibrated from time to time by comparing them with a higher-level generally agreed upon reference standard.

36 Stanford Hohauser, *Architectural and Interior Models* (New York: Van Nostrand Reinhold, 1970), 6.

37 W. R. Lethaby, *Architecture, Mysticism and Myth* (London: The Architectural Press, 1974), 1.

38 Ibid., 2.

39 *Oxford English Dictionary*, s.v. "demonstration."

40 *Oxford English Dictionary*, s.v. "divine." According to the Oxford Dictionary the etymology of the word *divine* comes not only from the Latin *divinus*, meaning pertaining to a deity, but also from the Latin *divinare*, which means to foretell or predict. Giambattista

Vico offers us an interesting insight into our relationship with the divine in his writings on the 'ideal eternal history'. He believed that humankind has gone through three phases of development called the divine age, the heroic age, and the human age. During the divine age, humans believed that everything was a god or was done or made by God.[a] This was an age of ritual semiosis with religious acts or divine ceremonies.[b] Vico notes that during this period humans communicated through divine hieroglyphics or by means of gestures or physical objects which had natural relations with the ideas.[c]

a   Giambattista Vico, *The New Science* (1725), trans. Thomas G. Bergin, and Max H. Fish, (Ithaca: Cornell University Press, 1984), 922.
b   Ibid., 929.
c   Ibid., 431.

41 *Oxford English Dictionary*, s.v. "sketch."
42 David A. Lauer, *Design Basics* (New York: Holt, Rinehart and Winston, 1979), 151.
43 Ibid.
44 Ibid.
45 See James J. Gibson, *Reasons for Realism: Selected Essays of James J. Gibson*, eds. E. Reed and R. Jones (New York: Lawrence Erlbaum Associates, 1982).
46 James J. Gibson, *The Ecological Approach to Visual Perception* (Boston: Houghton Mifflin Company, 1979), 275.
47 Merleau-Ponty, *The Primacy of Perception*, 183.
48 Gibson, *Reasons for Realism*.
49 "Questioned About First Sketches: Johann Peter Holzinger, Al Mansfold, Mario Botta, Hermann Fehling/Daniel Gogel, Alvaro Siza Vieira, James Stirling, Gottfried Bohm, Richard Meier, Helmut Striffler, Karljosef Schattner, Frank O. Gehry, Gustav Piechl, Walter M. Forderer, Gerd Neumann," *Daidalos* 5 (1982), 37.

50 Werner Oechslin, "The Well-Tempered Sketch," *Daidalos* 5 (1982), 103.
51 *Oxford English Dictionary*, s.v. "digital."
52 Branko Kolarevic, *Architecture in the Digital Age: Design and Manufacturing* (New York: Spon Press, 2003), 88.
53 Ibid., 91–92.

Choosing

Chapter 4

Design is about choices and
intentions, it is not accidental.
Design is about process. The end
user will usually not notice "the
design of it." It may seem like it
just works, assuming they think
about it at all, but this ease-of-use
(or ease-of-understanding) is not
by accident, it's a result of your
careful choices and decisions.

Garr Reynolds

Designers are required to make a great number of choices every day. You, as future architects, will be faced with choosing colors, materials, textures, forms, and many other important decisions that affect your designs.

It is unlikely that your experience in high school has given you the necessary skills to make

effective choices, which is why one of the primary goals of design school is to sharpen students' decision-making skills. Although choosing does not follow a formula and can be somewhat different for each individual or each situation, this chapter concerns how designers make choices about what is essential for their projects.

4.1 Codex Manesse

You might think that having a wide variety of choices is a good thing and that limiting or restricting your choices can lead to an unsatisfactory outcome. Consider what is involved in playing a game of chess. Is playing chess on a board of sixty-four squares overly restricting or does it help narrow the possibilities of moves to a manageable range that players can understand and engage with? Certainly, as a designer, you should consider a wide range of choices when making decisions. Being faced with too many choices can be overwhelming, however, and as a result you may regret not selecting an alternative. To make a good choice you must have an idea about what you need to decide in order to have something to judge against. For example, you might strongly believe in the work of an architectural movement and then judge your choices against those beliefs. Identifying with a proven paradigm can offer you a broad idea or main theme against which your other choices can be compared. Accepting such a foundation of beliefs is, of course, a choice in itself. You are probably now sensing a theme that has been discussed in previous chapters, the need to make good decisions and establish a repertoire of beliefs to judge those decisions against. Hopefully you recognize that this issue is vital to design and this is why we keep returning to it in various forms.

During studio, John, a first year student, grumbles to his classmates, "Why doesn't the professor ever tell us what she wants? How can we make sure that we're doing the project right?" Claire looks down at her project and says, "Yeah, there's so many choices that it gets confusing. Isn't there a guidebook to tell us what we should pick?" The studio teaching assistant Mika, standing nearby, hears all this and decides to enlighten the two. "While there are standards that will tell you how tall a hand rail needs to be or what size of beam to use, they won't help you with the actual design of the building. This studio is intended to put you in a position to learn about making choices. Since your projects probably won't be built you can make a few mistakes in your designs without major problems, but you need to get used to making decisions. The whole point of studio is to provide an environment where you can experiment and hone your decision-making skills."

"Have you ever heard about how Daedalus, the prototypical architect from Greek mythology, and his son Icarus escaped from the labyrinth? This story may help you to understand the responsibilities that you will face in your architectural career. Told in many versions, the story of their flight is basically this:

4.2 *The Fall of Icarus*

Daedalus was a very creative fellow and discovered a way that he and Icarus could escape from the labyrinth. Knowing that they could not escape on foot because the shores of Crete were well guarded, they found that the only way left was by air. Daedalus created enormous wings, made from wax and feathers and showed Icarus how to fly, but told him to keep away from the sun because the heat would melt the wax. Daedalus and Icarus escaped the labyrinth using the wings, but even though he had been warned, Icarus was too young and excited and was soon flying too close to the sun. His wings melted, and he fell into the sea and drowned.[1]

"The myth of Daedalus and Icarus is often understood as a warning to architects that they must be accountable when using technology and must build with restraint, responsibility, and care. The use of the term *technology* does not necessarily represent your new laptop or headphones, but rather the way people in our society provide themselves with material things in general."

Mika turns to leave, but adds, "You need to remember that your professors are attempting to educate you as future architects to be able to make wise decisions about the use of technology. This is because the technology of architecture affects so many lives – not only physically, but also spiritually. My question to you is, will the technology you create be developed through thoughtful, wise and responsible choices or will it be misused like Icarus' wings?" The question of technology helps introduce this chapter about choosing. The word architect comes from the combination of *archi*, which means "first or principal" and *tect*, a form of *tech*, meaning "technologist or technician."[2] As a scientific or industrial process, historically technology implied invention and innovation and more recently instrumental reason, requiring good judgment and active choosing.

JUDGING YOUR CHOICES

Choosing, by definition, is the mental process of judging the merits of multiple options and selecting one or more of them, and this is what we do when we design.[3] However, because architecture is so important to how we live, our choices must reflect good judgment, and this is one of the critical lessons you will learn in architecture school. In fact, for an architect, your ability to use good judgment in making decisions is one of the most important skills you can possess. Every day you will be required to make a wide range of important decisions directly affecting the way people will live in your buildings. Making good decisions requires confidence, clear thinking and the ability to be able to think through issues.

The action of judging means to form an opinion about something through careful weighing of evidence and the testing of premises,[4] and judgment is about creating balanced, just decisions. Lady Justice is a symbol of this concept. She is usually represented as a statue in front of courthouses and legal institutions carrying a sword, scales for weighing, and wearing a blindfold. Her scales represent a balanced process for rendering judgment, her sword suggests that justice can be swift and final, and the blindfold she wears symbolizes the philosophy that justice should be rendered "without passion or prejudice."[5] Lady Justice wears a Greco-Roman toga or tunic representing a long-standing civilization and

4.3 Fontaine de la Justice

historic philosophy. Similar to Lady Justice's scales, we are reminded of the flight of Daedalus and Icarus that recommends a balanced path through moderation. The word *moderate* means to be characterized by an avoidance of extremes of behavior.[6] Being moderate is keeping within reasonable or proper limits and not being extreme or excessive. Moderate is quite similar to the word *modest* meaning having a limited (and not exaggerated) estimate of one's ability or worth, lacking in vanity or conceit, or not bold or self-assertive.[7] Both words indicate freedom from exaggeration or overstatement, and help us to understand the concept of balance.[8]

Of course, architects also use scale, as mentioned in chapter three, as a standard of reference in measurement, and scale models that demonstrate conceptual thinking. But here we would like to introduce another connotation of scale in the sense of balance as demonstrated by Lady Justice. Another definition of scale can offer interesting insight into a meaning of architectural scale. Again, the word *scale* derives from the Latin *scalae*, which means ladder, and a further definition of scale can mean to climb. A scale can be a mechanism that provides an understandable balance between something that we know and something that we do not know.[9] A scale is also a device to calculate or measure proportion or ratio, and thus, acts as a comparator for judgment. The swift decisions of Lady Justice can speak of the importance of quickness in the decision-making process as was discussed in the last chapter. Ultimately, one can argue that your choices in architecture should be made without passion or prejudice since they can cloud your judgment.

There are many kinds of choices that you will be required to make as an architect. There are choices which can be made by any employee, those where there is only one obvious choice, those made by a collaborative decision, and those which can only be made by you because architects are central to the process. When choosing, you make a judgment about the quality of the options available. For the highly publicized design of the Parc de la Villette outside of Paris, the architect Bernard Tschumi presented a series of iterations concerning the design and layout of the site. Providing multiple options helps stimulate discussion, but at some point he was required to decide upon the best option so that the project could be constructed.

4.4 Parc de la Villette, Bernard Tschumi

Another downside is that presenting too many alternatives to public entities, such as city officials, may relegate important decisions to others. Being overly inclusive may also run the risk of having the project overly influenced by public opinion. By contrast, soliciting opinions, and participation, from the public can help gain acceptance for decisions that affect an entire community. As another example, in the 1970s the architect Charles Moore of the firm Moore Ruble Yudell used public television to petition public participation in the design of housing and community projects. After substantial input, the firm was able to analyze, weigh, and make decisions about what would eventually be built.

The reason for hiring architects is for their good judgment concerning the many choices needed to create a building. For example, when choosing materials with which to build you might think about cost, safety, ease of construction, or how the decisions support your main idea. Your choices about the materials will most likely be based on your judgment about how they will fill the needs of the project. Basically, you are arguing that your choices are the best possible to satisfy the needs of the project. However, all architecture cannot be approached the same way and thus other architects may disagree with your choices. Your buildings might then be part of an exchange of diverging views about what architecture is. As an architect, you may be asked to support the reasons for your ideas, actions, or theories. Using logical reasoning will help convey your intentions and convince others of your thinking. Statements with rational foundation will be more accepted than those based on personal opinion.

You may have already realized that in a studio critique your instructors will ask you to use reasoning and logic to justify your choices. They will ask you to use methods of reasoning such as comparison to precedent, definition, or inference, for example. The primary purpose is to teach you that your decisions should not be arbitrary, and the best decisions are based on solid reasoning. The ability to apply these skills early in your education will help them become ingrained in your thinking. Possibly later in your career, you will have acquired appropriate judgment and you will no longer need to justify your decisions in the same way. But recognize that throughout your entire career you will need to explain your reasoning and decisions to your clients and city ordinance boards, for example. Your professors are also teaching you that architectural design is not personal but instead based on thoughtful decisions and responsibility – consideration of what is best for your clients, the environment, the site, and all other external criteria. Also, you may soon realize that your professors are judging your project against your reasoning and specifically, your goals and criteria for the resolution of the project. Your statements concerning what you want the project to accomplish become part of the criteria in determining if you were successful. Your ability to bring your intentions in line with the solution (your project) makes the final outcome successful. Although these are not the only criteria, each project is multifaceted and may need to consider issues such as principles of design or successful use of precedent.

So how can you improve your ability to make good choices? You might ask yourself what choice makes the most sense, what is the main objective of your decision and then carefully judge from the variety of possible solutions. If the solution is elusive, you might study the pros and cons of the potential choices through diagrams, sketches, quick digital or physical study models. You might ask others such as your design instructor, fellow students, or friends about what they think of your choices. You might want to consider that many times you choose instinctively influenced by your personal beliefs and past experiences. Finally, you might improve your abilities in this area by surrounding yourself with others who consistently use good judgment when making decisions. This is why it is so important to study precedent by analyzing the works of accomplished architects. There are many invaluable library and online resources to help you in this regard. The ability to discuss projects and ultimately make appropriate decisions is one reason why the design studio is so important in your education as an architect. The studio environment gives you the opportunity to practice these skills. Inherently in this type of educational setting, you will make mistakes. It is important to remember that you are surrounded by teachers and fellow students who, hopefully, have an ability to help you make good design choices. It may not be surprising that you may learn more from your classmates and your own self-discovery than from your professors. The climate in the studio supports your learning but remember much of design education is based on your experiences.

Allowing others to provide their opinions on your project assists in viewing it from alternate perspectives. Although this can be helpful, sometimes too much input can be confusing. Of course when you have clients, it is important that they provide their opinions about various alternatives. It is critical to remember that in abdicating choice to others (rather than soliciting opinions) you must respect their choices. The Pritzker Prize winning architect Kevin Roche worked within a process used by Eero Saarinen where his assistants developed many alternatives to the commissions in the office. Once these projects were developed through the use of models and drawings, he could sufficiently visualize the projects and then come to a decision. In some instances, he provided the client a few options to engage them in the process of design. Dialogue such as this helps architects to better understand their client's needs and also creates trust and interaction that makes the process participatory. However, although Kevin Roche presented options to his clients, he was careful to put forward alternatives that he felt were appropriate and could be developed into a construction that would satisfy the needs of the program, the site, and his sense of design. In other words, giving someone else the ability to choose would forfeit his control of, and responsibility for, the project. This was especially critical because he was the one with the design education, skills, and experience, and the one who had the most information about the criteria and demands of the project.

SUPPORTING YOUR POSITION

In ancient Greece, Aristotle introduced the concept of rhetoric.[10] He explained how the framing of an argument was dependent upon five elements of structure – basically the style of the argument. Aristotle, also, advocated for the use of three aspects of persuasion: *logos*, *ethos*, and *pathos*.[11] These three classical tactics reveal a method to ensure a complete and convincing argument. He felt that of utmost importance was the ability to convince, not through facts, but persuasion. The Greeks felt that especially in matters of opinion, the construction (and thus, persuasion) of the argument was paramount.

In the studio, Song asks her professor about how to structure an argument. She says that in her family, her father always wins arguments because he is the biggest and talks the loudest. Song may be reminded of a more structured form of argument, the example of a debate. In an organized debate, two teams research an issue they will be able to advocate for or argue against. During the debate, each team attempts to discredit the other's argument and to find holes in the logic – looking for fallacy and ways to counter any premise. The teams base their presentation on authoritative material. Opinions are part of the argument, but the core of the debate is geared toward objective arguing and rational insight. They try to limit personal feelings, since each team hopes to win through factual evidence as a mode of persuasion.[12]

There are many ways people decide what is the appropriate way to come to a conclusion, for example, scientists know the appropriate research methods that stipulate the structure of experiments. As Song and her classmates discuss the many ways that different disciplines make decisions, they bring up examples of material testing, lawyers who need to argue a case in court, philosophers who may use methods of interpretation called *hermeneutics*, the role of detectives in criminal cases, or decisions made through elimination. In order to defend your choices you will want to learn about how to argue effectively. The following presents some suggestions about how to argue a position.

DEFENDING YOUR CHOICES

Perhaps the easiest way to argue an opinion is through the use of definition. You can usually convince an opponent as long as the two of you can agree on the parameters around what you are discussing.[13] It helps any disagreement to be able to adequately describe the thing you are talking about – explicitly and objectively. Less scientific methods of argument include those from cause and effect. This is a technique of persuasion by finding that one event caused another and its usage appeals to logical thinking. If one thing is true, then by inference and comparison so is the other. Another related method is argument from circumstance. In this case, you would be arguing that on the grounds that the solution is the most logical, no other course of action is practical or possible. In your writing courses, you may have been asked to present an argument from comparison, where you were required to contrast two opposing views. In studio, you may be asked to design in the style of a particular precedent. These are forms of argument by comparison.

A similar mode of argument is that of analogy, where it can be claimed that if things are alike in some respects, they are alike in other respects. Another type that is most likely familiar to you, and by far the most common, is an argument from evidence. In this instance, the two parties can convince through the use of facts, reference to authority, statistics, reports, and expert testimony.[14] These common methods can help you structure an argument, but how do they help you to decide? You can use these techniques when evaluating a problem, but be reminded that you may never be right. Instead the reasoning helps you to identify criteria that can assist you to locate better answers.

If making decisions is difficult, what things will help your ability to make informed and successful decisions? One way to focus is to use analysis. Many times in your education, and in your career, you will be requested to analyze information, but what does it mean to analyze something? As described briefly in chapter one pertaining to the study of precedent, a dictionary definition describes analysis as the separation of a whole into its component parts for individual study. This definition implies the study of such constituent parts and their interrelationships in making up a whole, and the work of inquiring into something thoroughly and systematically. Often analysis will make issues more clear and help reveal a correct way to proceed. Analysis in architecture is not merely showing photographs of what is being analyzed for comparison. Analysis is instead, the manipulation and transformation of images, texts, and information to really look at something more carefully and to understand it. Analysis requires action to re-present the information in a new way that helps to make that information more understandable.[15] Manipulation of this data may involve drawing over an image, cutting apart a plan, looking at the city as solids and voids, drawing again in high contrast, exaggerating pedestrian movement, highlighting paths, abstracting layers using a concept model, displaying symmetry, drawing exploded axonometric views, repeating salient features, accentuating patterns, and diagramming to name a few.

Diagrams can often help to analyze data in a way that makes the information useful; they are basically "a plan, sketch, drawing, or outline designed to demonstrate or explain how something works or to clarify the relationship between parts of a whole."[16] A chart or graph is an example of a good method to analyze data. Very successful examples of diagrams are subway maps. Fashioned after the iconic London Underground example, these maps make complex information easily understandable. Unlike other maps that seek to scale distances and represent physical features, subway maps are abstract. Possibly because they convey the tunnels underground, not seen by most of us, they can successfully generalize information in a graphic manner. Any curves of the tunnels are represented as straight lines. The maps show major geographical information and orientation but seldom provide specific landforms and features of the city. Their purpose is much more about orientation and

4.5 New York City subway map diagram

Choosing

general direction. Distances are often relative and do not necessarily represent the time traveled. The graphics emphasize relationships between things both below and above ground such as the stations. These stops and interchanges are identified with easy-to-read symbols. Although most use color to show the continuation of an uninterrupted tunnel, some reveal double lines or thickened lines to indicate train lines that run simultaneously (or on the same track).

Diagrams also generalize information to make a point not easily understood when presented in verbal form. In which case, architects and designers can use these diagrams to make a lasting impression or to express a concept they have trouble explaining. The sketch by the Spanish

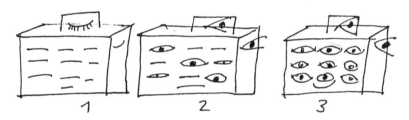

4.6 Offices for the Delegation of Public Health, Alberto Campo Baeza

architect Alberto Campo Baeza shows three conditions of openings for a building. Although it may have been easy for the architect to draw each opening as a window, the drawing alludes to windows as eyes and demonstrates the symbolic comparison of an eye with the view. This diagram also suggests that Baeza was concerned with the building's analogy to a person who sleeps and wakes – closing up for nighttime energy efficiency in contrast to daytime transparency. The second image shows an intermediate condition that may be the action of opening the building – not every eye at the same rate.

This diagrammatic sketch is also reminiscent of a way to think about openings in a building. It is often better not to use the word *window* when designing a façade. If you do, it is tempting to select a typical *window* that may not function the way you have intended. If you call the opening by terms that more closely describe what you want it to do you may be more successful in realizing its potential. In other words, a diagram can be quite specific and convey concepts that help to recall important issues in your design. In architecture, a graphic way to summarize or analyze information is vital to comprehending complex information. With techniques such as these, it may be productive to reconfigure the issue by using media to help think through decision-making.

In chapter two, it was suggested that to devise a concept you would need to prioritize your main objectives. The first part of making a decision might be to consider your objectives, alternatives, and the potential consequences of your decisions. In revisiting your goals, you can evaluate your choices in comparison to what you had initially decided was most important. It may be helpful to weigh your alternatives, and in doing so, you can explore the ramifications of your decisions. You may want to imagine the outcomes of several options. By quickly running through several scenarios, you can compare how each might culminate in a design solution. Obviously, thinking logically helps make reasoned decisions, while overly emotional conclusions or rash choices can keep you from making good decisions. You have most certainly been, at times, asked to think logically and these reasoned decisions emerge from thoughtful and measured analysis. Basically, logic is reasoning in a clear and consistent manner, so it takes time and careful consideration. Looking at something from a different perspective and hearing an opposing viewpoint is another way to think through a decision. You may want to solicit feedback from your professors, classmates, or experts, but sometimes you must listen to your instincts to help you view a solution more clearly. Mostly, it is important to weigh all aspects, avoid stereotypes, and evaluate your options.

Similar to the limits of play (see chapter three), you must construct boundaries to help you make decisions. As a designer, you make some of these *boundaries*, while others are outside of your control. Although we are using the term *boundaries*, some of these are more flexible than others. For example, the physics of gravity is a firm boundary, but you have options (a certain degree of subjectivity) as to how you utilize structure to reconcile gravity and where you place your building on a site. In another example, the program for your project may be set with square footage or square meter requirements – but it is important to recognize that a 100sq. ft. room can be 10' × 10' or 5' × 20' or 25' × 4' or be round, oval, or triangular. You have some ability to play within the rules, and thus boundaries can be firm and at the same time – vague. Within the precise lies the imprecise. Understanding which boundaries are firm and which can be altered may be vital to making informed decisions.

CRITERIA FOR CHOOSING

Both the boundaries provided for you, and the boundaries you set for yourself are based on criteria. The word *criteria* can be defined as a "standard for judging things by," thus, criteria can help architects and designers judge their designs.[17] With any architectural project, you will be confronted with criteria for design. Locating these criteria may involve extrapolating information from a client or could be presented to you in a program. The boundaries for decision making are part of those criteria and may include issues such as the building's orientation on a site, how many rooms and their function, qualities of light or a view, specific materials or construction methods, budget, and time frame, to mention a few. These conditions are the boundaries that help you frame your design and also make sure that the solution is successful.

Sonja and her classmates, after receiving the program for a building on an urban site, complain, "This site is so restrictive, we have no ability to make decisions. Why can't we design a building on a site free of zoning and such tight boundaries?" The professor thinks for a minute and he replies, "Where is it harder to design a building – in the middle of a desert or on the median strip of a highway?" After most of the class immediately indicate the median strip, the professor says, "I would disagree. A desert site has few features for you to react to. You could react to its horizontality and the sunrise and sunset, but devoid of interesting items for orientation it is very difficult to make

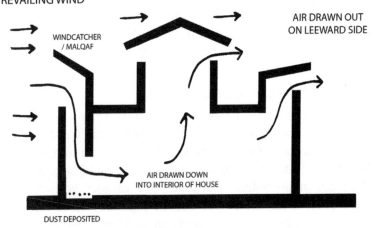

PREVAILING WIND

WINDCATCHER / MALQAF

AIR DRAWN OUT ON LEEWARD SIDE

AIR DRAWN DOWN INTO INTERIOR OF HOUSE

DUST DEPOSITED

4.7 A diagram showing the principle of a malqaf or windcatcher for natural ventilation in traditional Arabic architecture

decisions. The median strip is difficult because it is narrow, but because of the boundaries, you can react to the narrowness and the linearity in interesting ways." Sonja and her classmates then realize that maybe total freedom is not a good thing.

As stated above, criteria that form boundaries for a design project can be those that we describe as needs. Other program items that dictate boundaries might be zoning, building codes, sustainability, financial restrictions, structural properties, physics, climate, sun angles, and restrictions of the human body. These functional items of a program fulfill the physical requirements of a building, but any architectural designer should ask whether the building brings inspiration to those who inhabit it. Architecture, rather than mere building, should be functional but also exhibit qualities that will satisfy people's need to be inspired by their surroundings. So how can you define the client's needs? A perfect view, a feeling of security, an inviting space – are these client needs? Absolutely: the experiential qualities of a building are fundamental.

If restrictions stipulate the form of a building, how much opportunity do architects have to make decisions when designing? Returning to a former example, you are given a specific site and you recognize that this is a boundary that you must adhere to, but how you choose to locate your building on that site can happen in myriad ways. In other words, respect your boundaries, but also recognize that they have inherent flexibility. Sonja's professor stops the studio and says, "Let me give you an example of the flexibility of play and boundaries with a story about the artist Marcel Duchamp."

Marcel Duchamp, the founder of the Dadaist art movement, was well known for his aesthetic study of machines. After producing many of his machines,

Duchamp found himself spending more and more of his time playing chess. In fact, he became so accomplished at the game that during the 1930s he actually represented his country as a member of the French championship chess team. These two interests of Duchamp's were not mutually exclusive; he viewed them as quite similar. He wrote that he found many points of resemblance between his art and chess: "In fact, when you play a game of chess it is as if you were sketching something, or as if you were constructing the mechanism by which you would win or lose. The competition part of the business has no importance, but the game itself is very, very plastic, and it is probably that which attracts me."[18]

4.8 Marcel Duchamp and John Cage chess match

In a way, your architectural designs are similar to the playing pieces of an intricate game, and like the game of chess your designs can be engaged differently each time you play. The purpose of this game is to discover the truth about the best way to build for the ways people live. Each time we create a piece of architecture it can be used to see whether the current rules of the game are well defined. However, occasionally a rule might be found lacking and will be changed through the mutual consent of the players.

As discussed in chapter two, your conceptual ideas also guide the decisions you make in designing your project. Your concept contains artificial criteria that you impose upon yourself. These criteria are not arbitrary but pertain to the project at hand. You establish the concept based on a set of beliefs or some issues important to the project. The decisions that led to your concept were not arbitrary, but they were artificial. Arbitrary and artificial are not the same thing. Arbitrary is random, and certainly your concept was not a random decision. But your concept was artificial since you dictated the direction of the project. Again, concepts are guiding principles that give your project life, and thus, soul.

Other criteria that will help you make decisions during the life of a project are those that involve ethics and responsibility. You must act with honesty and integrity, adhere to confidentiality, and have solid and respectable personal characteristics. These responsibilities extend to ethical questions such as making your architecture as good and well thought out as possible. The word *ethical* speaks of a set of principles of right conduct, and is a theory or a system of moral values.[19]

Not identical, but related, are your responsibilities for professional ethics. In your role as a designer, you assume leadership as the person responsible for protecting humans and designing good spaces for them to live, work, and enjoy. This represents a huge responsibility and the architecture profession takes protecting the health, safety, and welfare of the public very seriously.[20] Much of this involves the registration and licensure of architects, but a professional attitude also involves listening to the clients, finishing projects in a timely manner, observing confidentiality, giving objective advice, fully informing everyone, making a complete set of drawings, utilizing new information systems, and all the other ethical practices that are expected of you. As an example, there are two criteria that all architects must adhere to in various ways: social responsibility and sustainability. Responsibilities to society include environments for humans and also doing everything possible for humanity. It is also your ethical responsibility to design in an environmentally responsible way and to inform yourself and your clients of the ramifications of different building techniques and the use of various materials. The UIA, an international architects' association, uses the term *Responsible Architecture*. They define this architecture as showing concern for sustainability, professional practice, and social responsibility.[21] With so many issues to worry about, architects and designers need to prioritize in order to focus on what is important.

FILTERING AND FOCUSING THE CHOICES

Zoe has come up with a number of concepts for her art gallery project, but is finding it hard to decide which one is the best because she likes them all equally. Her professor suggests creating a list of core requirements that the project needs, and comparing each concept to the list to see which one is most appropriate. He suggests that while all of her concepts may work on some level, after comparing them to her criteria, one might reveal itself as more appropriate for the current situation. He tells her it's sort of like natural selection. For example, before industrialization in England, white moths were the most common because they were easily able to camouflage on the light-colored trees. After the pollution of industrialization, however, the trees darkened, and predators were easily able to spot the white moths, so the darker moths began to flourish.[22] The type of moth that

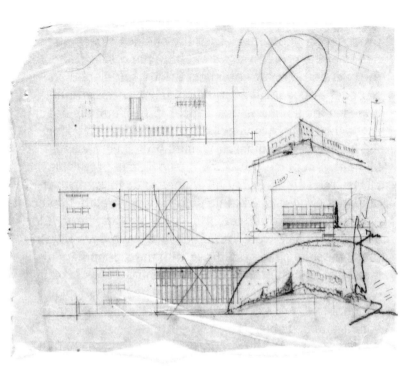

4.9 Library and office building of Salman Schocken, sketches, Erich Mendelsohn

survived depended on which one was most appropriate for the current situation.

Criteria are important in making choices. Just like a sieve, you can filter your ideas through your criteria and see what comes out in the end. Unnecessary elements can be discarded, and you can end up with a clearer and more focused concept. Think of a decanter used for wine. Wine poured into a decanter is left to rest so that sediment and other natural impurities settle at the bottom of the vessel. The clear liquid at the top is then poured off and the sediment remains in the decanter. This creates a purer, more enjoyable wine.

Architects and designers may find that after a similar process, the good choices (or the choices closest to the needs of the project) stand out from the rest. A sketch by the twentieth-century architect Erich Mendelsohn shows a process of evaluation and elimination as he graphically chooses the solutions that appear to best suit his needs at the time. What we view is a page of alternatives for the façade of a commercial building. In several cases, Mendelsohn places an "X" by unsuccessful proposals and circles the solutions that he wishes to develop further. He does not choose one at this point, but several that could be amalgamated and refined into a final building form. After all the proposals were viewed he may have been filtering the choices to single out those with the most potential. Likewise, after spending time with your idea, as explained in chapter three, you need to remove any parts of your concept than are extraneous, so that it is as clear and concise as possible.

One form of filtering is deductive reasoning, which most people know from the Sherlock Holmes stories by Sir Arthur Conan Doyle. Also known as top-down logic, deductive reasoning involves taking a general statement and using it to reach a specific conclusion. For example, given that all bachelors are unmarried males, and given that the person in question is a bachelor, it can be deduced that the person is an unmarried male.[23] Deductive reasoning is contrasted by inductive reasoning, which evaluates general propositions gained from specific examples.

The first step in deduction is the sifting of information, as "it is of the highest importance in the art of detection to be able to recognize of a number of facts which are incidental and which vital."[24] This skill could be especially useful for you because while most aspects of an idea may

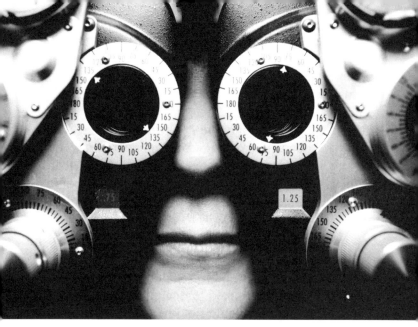

4.10 Cmdr. Amy Burin is fitted to a phoropter

work, there may be others that need to be discarded in order to adhere to the predetermined boundaries. Like a stonemason, students must be able to chip away at their big ideas so that the pieces of their idea fit perfectly with the requirements.

Once an idea has been filtered through a set of boundaries, the resulting concept becomes much more focused. The word *focus* comes to us directly from the Latin word *focus*, related to a hearth or fireplace. It's interesting that the origins of these words are architectural terms referring to the center of the home. When one is focusing they are looking for the center, core, heart, hub, or target. For design students, your focus should concentrate on the center of your design, the big idea. The focus can mean a center of activity, attraction, or attention. Most importantly, for you as a designer, is the definition of focus as the state or condition permitting clear perception or understanding. As mentioned in chapter one, perceiving is to become aware of, know, or identify by means of the senses. When you clarify, you make something free of confusion so that it becomes understandable. So we can argue that focusing, for a designer, is about finding and clarifying the main concept of your design. This is an ongoing process because your main concept may at first be fuzzy, out of focus, and unclear. Anyone who wears corrective lenses understands the importance that focus has, for without them, their vision is blurry and it is difficult to see details clearly.

A concept can often be out of focus when you first start a project. In fact, you need to understand that much of what we work on as architects is out of focus at first. For example, you may be asked to design an art gallery, but in the beginning you would not know what that specific gallery would be like. It is the job of architects to be able to continually focus an idea to concentrate on its core essentials. Much like the process of distillation, where a substance is heated to a vapor and then condensed to extract the pure essence, ideas must constantly be taken apart, the impurities removed, and then the main concepts brought back together. The one major difference, however, is that while the parts that do not work may be removed from one project, they can be reused in another project where they are more appropriate. As Zoe's professor suggested, one project may favor light moths, while another may require those that are dark.

Erin is sitting in the studio confused about how to proceed. The professor stops by and asks how he can help her get started. Erin replies, "I think I need to go to the library, I still do not know enough about the retreat for the artist that I am expected to design. I am not sure enough about the artist's work, skills, or history." The professor stops Erin, "You have been studying this artist's work for weeks and prepared a successful presentation to the class, I believe you know enough to begin to design. In any situation, you will never know everything you need to know. It is vitally important, especially when you are a professional, to know when and who to ask. Comprehending your skills, and recognizing your limitations, is key to being successful. This is the reason that architects employ experts and consultants at different stages of a project. Since the profession will change drastically in your lifetime you will need to continually learn, hone your skills, and find new knowledge. But in any project, once you have gained a 'reasonable' amount of knowledge, you must proceed on faith and trust your decisions. It is important to consider the meaning of *abductive* reasoning."

Abductive reasoning is a term that originates with the philosopher and semiotician Charles Sanders Peirce.[25] Recognizing that there are things we will never know completely, Peirce viewed abduction as a form of logic where humans can utilize data and establish a hypothesis that attempts to explain the importance of that evidence. Abduction can be interpreted as educated guessing.[26] Once you know as much relevant information as possible, you need to draw conclusions based on your interpretation of the facts and what is reasonable to assume. For example, if you are walking along in the city and feel the ground rumbling beneath you, you could make an educated guess as to what the cause is. You could think of a number of causes such as an earthquake or giant subterranean worms, but since you know that there is a subway line running beneath the road, the most likely cause of the rumbling is that subway cars are passing underneath you. You will never know anything for certain unless you explore further, but you must proceed with your best knowledge.

In architecture, the only thing absolute may be the existence of gravity – and architects are currently questioning this notion! So you must make your best educated guess, knowing that the choices are not necessarily right or wrong, but bad, good, and better. You can never have all the information possible, but at some point you must make a decision, take a leap of faith, and commit to an idea.

DOUBTING YOUR CHOICES

One of the most difficult tasks for students is to proceed with confidence. Doubt can cause stagnation and the inability to progress in a design. Xuemei's professor stops by her desk and asks why she isn't drawing or modeling her project. Xuemei replies, "I am not sure if my concept is on the right track, I am afraid to proceed because I may be wrong – I have too many ideas. Everyone else seems to have good ideas and are starting to make models." Doubt is a huge problem – everyone has doubts, and since design requires so many decisions it is easy to become overwhelmed with indecision and insecurities. Every architect has doubts, although they seldom admit them. Remember that much time can be wasted pulling out your hair, spinning your wheels, or avoiding moving the project forward – because of doubt. The professor continues, "Xuemei, do not worry, you must proceed with confidence. The only way to find out if your idea is on the right track is to work on development. Although you may find out later that you are going in the wrong direction, you can only discover this through action."

The professor asks Xuemei to explain her thinking and why she is stymied. As she explains that she has twenty models and lots of thoughts about different directions, the professor stops her and says, "You may have too many ideas. How can you prioritize – how can you focus on one strong idea and let everything else fall into place? Remember that you will be practicing until you are 100 years old – find the idea that is most appropriate for this project using your stated criteria and save the other ideas for another project. You do not need to put everything that you know and believe into this one – streamline your thinking to the most important issues at this time. Because designing a building is so complex, when you further develop the project you will be using all your skills and knowledge to put the building together."

Returning to a former analogy, think of a game of chess. You cannot save all your pieces and win the game. By giving up certain pieces at strategic times you can gain an advantage. Most importantly, you are sacrificing a piece to get into a better position to achieve your goals – giving up the pawn might put you in the right position to take your opponent's queen. Thus, as a designer you need to focus, filter, and make choices that further your primary design goal. You also need to realize that your concept is the theme and acts as a language. If your project is speaking French, inserting another visual language can cause your project to be perceived as incongruent and disorderly.

Chapter three concentrated on playing with various media and this chapter has encouraged strategies for choosing. Although it is you who ultimately arrives at the decisions important to your project, you can make better choices through careful consideration of all the factors involved. Many of you put off choosing for as long as possible hoping the answers will become clearer with time. Actually, the earlier you make decisions the sooner you can evaluate to see if you are on the right track. Similar to the story about Xuemei, it may seem easier to continue to research and play with your media. This tendency may be the reason so many students end up working on their projects until the minutes before they are due. Remember that decision making does not get easier in the professional world, but you must learn to believe in yourself and the validity of your criteria to progress through the process. When practicing, there are other factors that make coming to conclusions imperative: financial constraints, responsibility to the other players in the process such as consultants and contractors, and often the necessity of client needs. Although this book sets out broad time-lines of processes for projects in school, fast-tracked construction or simultaneous processes such as BIM will change the way buildings are delivered. And as you will experience with your projects while in school, none progress in an identical manner nor do they each follow a linear or comparable pattern. You may envision that choosing implies completion. On the contrary, *choosing* leads to opportunities for further definition and evaluation. As stated in the Opening chapter, a typical process involves a spiral evolution of problem, solution, and critique that happens continually while a project is being designed.

Endnotes

1. There are a great many sources for information on the myth of Daedalus. We recommend Thomas Bulfinch, *The Age of Fable* (New York: The Heritage Press, 1942).
2. *The Compact Edition of the Oxford English Dictionary* (Oxford: Oxford University Press, 1971), s.v. "architect."
3. *Oxford English Dictionary*, s.v. "choose."
4. *Oxford English Dictionary*, s.v. "judging."
5. The phrase "without passion or prejudice" has uncertain origins as it shows in numerous legal documents, notably in *Remarks on the Address of Sixteen Members of the Assembly of Pennsylvania* by Pelatiah Webster in 1787.
6. *Oxford English Dictionary*, s.v. "moderate."
7. *Oxford English Dictionary*, s.v. "modest."
8. *Oxford English Dictionary*, s.v. "balance."
9. Albert C. Smith, *Architectural Model as Machine* (Oxford: Architectural Press, 2004), xxx.
10. See Aristotle, *The Art of Rhetoric*, trans. John Henry Freese (Cambridge, MA: Harvard University Press, 1926).
11. Ibid.
12. See Leslie Phillips, William Hicks, and Douglas Springer, *Basic Debate* (Glencoe/McGraw-Hill, 2001) and Robert E. Dunbar, *How to Debate* (Scholastic Library Publishing, 1994).
13. Maxine Hairston, *A Contemporary Rhetoric* (Boston: Houghton Mifflin Company, 1978), 212–226.
14. Ibid., 227–236.
15. *Oxford English Dictionary*, s.v. "analysis."
16. Ibid.
17. *Oxford English Dictionary*, s.v. "criteria."
18. Calvin Tomkins, *The Bride and the Bachelors* (New York: Viking Press, 1965), 9–10 and Smith, *Architectural Model as Machine*, 82–83.
19. *Oxford English Dictionary*, s.v. "ethical."
20. "American Institute of Architects," www.aia.org.
21. "Union Internationale Des Architectes," uia-architectes.org.
22. See Carol R. Ember, Melvin Ember, and Robert D. Hoppa, *Physical Anthropology and Archaeology* (Guilford: Prentice Hall, 2006).
23. Hairston, *A Contemporary Rhetoric*, 248–280.
24. Quote from Sir Conan Doyle, in the story "The Reigate Puzzle," in Umberto Eco and Thomas A. Sebeok, eds., *Sign of Three: Dupin, Holmes, Peirce* (Indiana University Press, 1988), 65.
25. Justus Buchler, *Philosophical Writings of Peirce* (New York: Dover Publications, 1955), 98–119. Also see Eco and Sebeok, *Sign of Three*.
26. Ibid.

Defining

Chapter 5

Design [is] the emerging ethos formulating and then answering a very new question: What shall we do now, in the face of the chaos that we have created?

John Hockenberry

As discussed in chapter three, architectural design starts with making a mark and an idea as to how to construct a building. The art historian Ernst Gombrich writes about the role of meaning and intention in the first appearance of architecture. He suggests that buildings were conceived to keep the rain off our heads and help us stay warm in the winter but also served to keep away the unknown things that frighten us. It is important in this chapter to build on previous discussions of how architecture is reflective of a society's norms. Because architecture is so important to how people live it has a major impact in defining their culture and the ways they inhabit buildings. Though architecture from different historical periods may appear physically quite similar, there can be major cultural differences as to what these buildings were seen as defining. For example the Great Pyramid at Giza might help define ancient Egypt while the glass pyramid at the Louvre represents modern France. These buildings may each represent what is important to that society but their purpose as a memory device or cultural icon is vastly different. So we can see that architecture can be used to help define a culture's goals and ideals. But what can be meant by definition? The *Oxford English Dictionary* contains the etymological root of the word *definition,* revealing that it originates from the Latin word *definire,* meaning the setting of bounds or limits.[1] Again, we return to a discussion of boundaries, because to define something is to establish boundaries in order to designate meaning. We are also reminded

5.1 Khafre's pyramid from the pyramid of Khufu, Giza

that the word *designate* is closely related to the word *design,* meaning to mark out. A part of defining is the action of describing. It is difficult to describe anything that is too ambiguous or open-ended. Describing your projects through drawings or models is critical to making your concept known to yourself and others. Thus, defining and describing are interconnected in the design process.

This chapter concentrates on aspects of design that are related to *definition.* After focusing on what is essential, it is important to understand the qualities and ramifications of the choices that have been made and to continue to refine and clarify. Design does not begin with definition nor does it end with early decisions. Definition is an extension of choosing and editing and it helps architects and designers to describe a decision.

In their design studio, Jamal and Emily are working on a public housing project that involves various units on a large site. Jamal's project is beginning to resemble a commune, where the families that will occupy the housing will

5.2 Pyramid Arena at Front Street in Memphis

share eating and food preparation areas. He feels this organization is more efficient and accounts for the ways people like to be socially interactive when dining. He has a few spare minutes and stops by Emily's desk. She is placing various small pods across the site. Her solution emphasizes the autonomy of the family unit. Jamal notices the differences between the two projects and begins to understand what his professors meant when they said that architects and designers define how people will live through their designs.

When architects design they develop a plan or drawing to show the look and function of a building. In the strictest of terms, designing is the art or action of conceiving of and producing a plan or drawing of something before it is made.[2] When you design you must decide upon the look and function of a building or other object by making a detailed drawing or model of it. As you have seen in chapter four, to design a building you need to make many choices, for example you must decide what materials to build with, how it will interact with nature, and what form it should take.

There are a great many rules involved in making a good definition. As an example of these rules, a definition must indicate the essential characteristics of the thing being defined. As philosophers speculate, a thing can be a material or inanimate object or it can be a matter of concern, deed, act, or accomplishment that exists as a separate entity.[3] Things can be distinguished from what is purely an object of thought since a thing need not be precisely designated. It can be an artistic composition and as such, a building conceived as architecture or an architectural scale model can be a thing used for creating definition. Your models and drawings as mechanisms for thinking, for example, help you understand your project and thus assist you to define the boundaries of your solution.

Words take on new meaning and concepts evolve over time, especially with new information and usages. Some evolve because of slang such as *cool* and *bad*. Other words change because society needs to find similar words to describe new products such as a computer mouse. The

Oxford English Dictionary is constantly adding new words to its volumes. Most of these are hybrids that combine or reconstitute definition, giving new meaning in the reassignment. Likewise, definitions of things are constantly changing as we find new meaning in the objects that we make. The primary function of definition is to present meaning for things that are not clearly understood in a context of things that are clearly understood. Definitions present the intended meaning and offer a description of a thing's fundamental characteristics. They increase comprehension, impart information, and attempt to prevent ambiguity and imprecision.[4] They are resolutions, and as declared intentions they indicate how to use a thing in a specific manner. When discussing the transitory qualities of definition, the philosopher John W. Miller points out that, "A static definition is neither experimentally nor logically possible ... we are compelled therefore to search for a relative permanence, and we find that definition as a whole changes in respect to other definitions."[5]

A definition may be compared to a paradigm, and as mentioned earlier, paradigms or belief systems shift depending upon influences of culture and world events. New technologies and methods of construction also change definitions of building and architecture. As architects and designers know, advances in technology, how people live, and the requirements for buildings affect the ways buildings both look and perform. If this was not so, you would not need to study architectural history. Actually, history changes also. We would imagine that what has been written down is fact, but history is really interpretation and speculation about artifacts and texts. History significantly changed when travelers discovered an iceman frozen in the Italian Alps for thousands of years. When scientists inspected tools found with him, historians realized that the Bronze Age began earlier than they had previously believed. This new information altered a previously static paradigm.

Definitions are also hard to specifically articulate. When trying to define a word for example, there is not always a clear parallel. Instead, to define you may need to explain what something is like, what it is not like, and other words that have similar meaning. Usually, you need to talk around the meaning hoping that with many examples the true or accurate definition can become clear. This example, of surrounding an exact definition with those that are close, also makes finding a definition difficult. Since definitions change with societies' reinterpretation, absolute definitions are constantly moving targets. Most definitions are collective, meaning they are understood or agreed upon as true by a large group of people. Definitive meanings mutate, whether they are definitions of words, interpretation of images, examples from history, or concepts. The philosopher Jean Baudrillard, in his book *Simulations*, discusses how evolution in the repetition of images or events becomes *simulacra*. He writes that images change meaning each time they are repeated, and this change in meaning occurs often just in the action of repetition.[6]

It may be useful to examine a more recent architectural example in order to reflect upon the ramifications of *simulacra*. An example of the utilization of the traditional Greek model can be seen today in Nashville, Tennessee. The city was, at one time, known as the "Athens of the South" because of its many schools, colleges, and its accompanying culture. In 1897, a full-scale plaster model of the Parthenon was constructed (meant to last only one year) in the city to commemorate the Tennessee Centennial Exposition. However, the plaster Parthenon quickly became representative of the city and its culture, and consequently

5.3 Replica of the Parthenon in Centennial Park, Nashville

it was not removed. Benjamin Franklin Wilson III, in *The Parthenon of Pericles and its Reproduction in America*, writes:

> In this age of eager restlessness, constant experiment and changing fashions, it is essential that we should have some standards of the beautiful preserved to us that are beyond question or criticism. Such a standard existed in the Parthenon at Athens, and the people of America and of the world are indeed fortunate in its reproduction at Nashville, where it stands as a beacon light to man and woman of every land who are interested in the culture of the past, the present, or the future.[7]

To the citizens of Nashville, the Parthenon represented a standard of perceived excellence, general stability, and moderation. Wilson writes, "'The Greeks in Pericles' day did not allow the imagination to run away with them. Every detail of the Parthenon, every line, bears silent witness to their moderation. They abhorred eccentricity. One of their proverbs, 'no excess', is exemplified by the perfect harmony of the proportion of the Parthenon."[8]

The building of the Nashville plaster Parthenon does not, on the surface, appear very unusual. More permanent copies of Greek temples serve as banks, courthouses, and academic buildings. The intention in building the plaster Parthenon was to demonstrate that the future of Nashville was one based on moderation, idealism, and stability. However, when this situation is viewed more closely certain contradictions begin to appear. Certainly the residents of late-nineteenth-century Nashville did not believe mere plaster would provide the city with a bright future. It was the form of the Parthenon that represented the builder's intentions. However, as the architectural historian George Hershey has noted, the Greek temple's form derived from somewhat wild and pagan roots, which would most likely have scandalized the population of Nashville.[9] This is probably, in part, why the garish colorful decorations were not reproduced in Nashville: the bright colors would have been considered excessive. It can be noted then, that the meaning of the Parthenon changed depending upon its context and its original meanings may have actually been forgotten. Its meaning is subject to shifts and can hardly be considered stable. The plaster Parthenon became representative of the city and its future. However, soon after it was built, the Nashville Parthenon began to deteriorate, for plaster is not a very stable material. By 1931 the crumbling plaster Parthenon began to represent an embarrassment for Nashville and was finally replaced by a more permanent concrete replica. This copy of the copy replaced the unstable, shifting representation of stability, moderation, and idealism. This is an example of a *simulacrum*. When the original reasons behind a defining concept, such as those setting the form of a Greek temple, become unclear or forgotten, a *simulacrum* may occur.

The word *simulacrum* comes from the Latin word *simulare*, which means to make like or to simulate. A simulacrum is a representation, image, or effigy having merely the form or appearance of a certain thing without possessing its substance or proper qualities. It can be an imitation or sham, which can create a superficial likeness, appearance, or semblance.[10] The Nashville Parthenon in its repetition and shifting meaning is also reminiscent of how ideas of postmodern images and imagination have taken on new connotations. Aesthetic philosophers relate how images change meaning through their distribution in the mass media. We continually see the iconic images of Leonardo Da Vinci's Mona Lisa distorted for commercialization, obviously assigned new meaning in its transformation.[11]

5.4 Mona Lisa tagged

To further explain, the etymological roots of the words *define* and *design* may be a way to help understand how you need to define and describe your projects after you have chosen a direction. Again, as stated in earlier chapters, for architects and designers, designing is not solely choosing aesthetic form but rather uniting the function, construction, and beauty of a project.[12] The word *design* emerges from the Middle French *desseign*, meaning purpose or project, from the Italian *disegno*, and from the Latin *disegnare*, as we saw with designate, to mark out.[13] Other related origins of the word include concepts of designing as scheming, the action of pointing out or marking out, or design as a device or specification. It is interesting to note that during the Italian Renaissance the term *disegno* was used for a formal discipline of design that involved representing ideal form. It suggests that an idea is intentional and that idea requires experience and production. The artists of the Renaissance understood that *disegno* was a different function of the mind than observation.[14]

> In the vita of Luca della Robbia, Vasari, speaking of the "arts of design," assures the reader that "whoever has the clear idea of what he desires to produce in his mind ... will ever march confidently and with readiness towards the perfection of the work which he proposes to execute." "Idea" and disegno, one notices, are here used interchangeably. If we accept this interpretation of disegno, the "arts of design" can only mean the arts that flow from the images in the maker's mind. ... But in Vasari's thought disegno also has a different meaning, one that is closer to what we now understand by this term: a linear configuration indicating the structure of what is represented and the production of which requires skill, dexterity, and training.[15]

It is then easy to speculate that defining an ideal form is part of the act of designing. So to design and define are similar and can help you to understand that every part of the process contains the actions of design, not only the first imaginative motions. A critical part of design is to define what is important and move forward. An example about architectural practice may help to explain the importance of definition to the design process.

Hilary and her classmates are having problems understanding how defining is part of architecture and design. They go to the library and also begin to look online to try and get a handle on this elusive concept. In their research they find that to define a project architects use various methods to organize and define the scope of the project. Although not things that they will encounter until they are in the later years of their education, in the early stages of a design time-line, architects must interview their clients to identify the needs and desires for the intended building. They also realize that the designers must research the accurate boundaries of the site through surveys or city records and identify what they do not know about the program, such as requirements for the flooring of a dance studio. Early stages also define the budget and decide on an appropriate time-line for design development and construction. Some of the many issues to accomplish early are applications for permits and deciding the conceptual approach. All of these activities put parameters around the scope of the project and begin to define what the project will be. Hilary soon realizes that in the early years of her schooling, she does not need to know all these legal or technical requirements. But this research helps her to understand how her actions at the beginning of the project frame the way the project processes. Her choice of cardboard or the methods she uses to draw can determine the next steps. She also understands that many of these tasks continue to evolve and are revisited as the process progresses, but that definition solidifies the things that are unknown.

Two examples may demonstrate this idea. Vincent Scully, when analyzing the work of Paul Rudolph, speculates that his drawing technique of hatched lines evolved into the vertically striated concrete that he used so much.[16] In another example, certain computer programs make some moves easier than others. It has been said that projects designed in Form Z take on a certain similarity in form. It is important to be conscious of the media and techniques used to establish definition. You can practice these skills by learning mechanisms to help you clarify the decisions necessary to complete your project.

CLARIFYING

Carlos has been toying with parts of his project; they seem so disparate and are not making sense to him. He heads home after studio still thinking about the project and why it bothers him so much. The next day his professor stops by to view his progress. Still feeling off balance, he entreats his professor for advice. The professor proceeds to tell a story. "Pretend that, when you are a practitioner, you are called away on an emergency. How do you ensure that your employees or colleagues will finish your project as you envisioned it? By imbuing the project with a system, solutions to questions along the way can be resolved by adhering to the order as it was originally conceived." The professor continues by asking Carlos if he has always taken apart things to see how they work. When Carlos nods in astonishment the professor affirms that this is a trait of designers to always try to understand things that are not initially clear. As discussed earlier, the human mind continually searches for order in a world of chaos. Our minds try to make sense of things that seem cryptic, ambiguous, or irrational, which is why we often feel off-balance until we find rational answers. Architects and designers employ precision to control things that are abstract or undefined. This exactness or accuracy helps find the specifics of a project and refines areas that are vague. Although most designers feel initially off-balance, order for designers may provide the logic, patterns, or rhythms that assist them to make the project understandable, and these are certainly the precision of defining and refining the details. The architectural theorist Anthony C. Antoniades writes that order is "the quality of a work of architecture which tells the user or the observer that there are not inequities in the organization of the elements and that, therefore, an equilibrium, or balance, is at hand." He goes on to write that this order can be described as having few "conflicts."[17] But what does this mean?

Since this chapter concerns definition, it is appropriate to return to the dictionary definition that *clarity* is "to make clear of confusion or uncertainty, or to elucidate."[18] The action of clarifying has connotations of removing impurities and making something clean. This definition has religious overtones and may imply a transition from being contaminated or sinful to a more moral position. The word *pure* certainly suggests principles of proper and ethical conduct, but it also connotes truth and perfection. To continue a logical progression of meaning, *perfection* indicates beauty and order. To *perfect* is a process of getting closer to perfection, since with an absence of flaws something perfect must be considered beautiful. Having already discussed beauty at some length, the concept of order needs some reflection in relationship to clarity. German philosopher Gotthold Ephraim Lessing writes that, "for me the greatest beauty always lies in the greatest clarity." As philosophers have felt that order and beauty are connected, order and harmony have similarities. The architect and theorist, Frank Ching, states that order is "a condition of logical, harmonious or comprehensible arrangements in which each element of a group is properly disposed with reference to other elements and to its purpose."[19] Order often utilizes geometries and number systems to organize the parts of a whole, where harmonies reveal complex relationships in music, but also in visual systems. Order also assists architects and designers to clarify their ideas; when things are put in place they are easier to understand. Ordering systems help architects because construction is to assemble and form elements in a way that creates shelter for people. Building techniques depend upon order. The assembly of a roof, for example, requires the repetition and regular spacing of the beams. Although some buildings

5.5 Labyrinth on the portico of the cathedral of San Martino at Lucca

do not use traditional structural elements, the digital applications still compute order, even if it is now more complex. Part of architecture is an attempt to define nature to understand it and give it an order so that it can be comprehended. There are many instances, through history, where people have tried to define nature through architecture. Some distinctive examples of this include the Pantheon in Rome as a representation of the universe, and the labyrinth of Greek mythology.[20] In Greek mythology, Daedalus was responsible for building a labyrinth for King Minos. In Medieval times, the labyrinth was given sacred connotations and it symbolized the difficult path to find God. Similarly, labyrinths served as symbolic forms of pilgrimage. Labyrinthine carvings on the floor of Gothic cathedrals may also be interpreted to refer to the complexities of the Church's construction. These buildings may be seen as monuments that define the boundless and help to locate order in nature. The labyrinth continues to represent our search for order or understanding of a chaotic world.

Another way to think about finding order and definition by creating boundaries is an example of a first year student, Andrew, who is uncertain about the word *space*. The upper year students seem to understand what it is, and he thought he knew what the word meant. But after a design review that referred to architectural space, Andrew is not sure he can define it. With some research and contemplation, he realizes that architectural space is space that has constructed elements to define it. In other words, placing walls around volumes of air orders and differentiates that space from other spaces. This action is intentional and shows that an architect is clearly designating that space for a specific function. This also means that through bounding, clarifying, and defining the space as architectural it is also being designed to feel a certain way. The boundaries of architectural space do not need to be four walls and a roof, however. Architectural space can be bound partially and still convey implied space. Just as a line of columns implies a wall, other barriers imply an architectural space. A project by Kazuyo

Sejima and Ryue Nishizawa for the Serpentine Gallery Pavilion in London shows a roof supported by slender columns. Although not enclosed with walls, this project represents architectural space since it is an intentionally designed space for people with a specific function. The space is covered with a roof, and when people are under the roof they feel they are within a designated (designed) space. Although it may be necessary to imply enclosure, architectural space is more dependent upon how the space is perceived.

5.6 The 2009 Summer Pavilion at the Serpentine Gallery in Kensington Gardens

DEVELOPING

In Kara's studio everyone has identified a concept that has been well considered and has been experimenting with media. Now it is time to apply those beginnings to the project at hand. The students in the studio need to develop those explorations into a cohesive project. Kara's professor encourages the class to design their project, but everyone is already happy with their project as it is. Kara says, "I have played with media and I am afraid that I will ruin the project by making it real. It has so much possibility right now." The professor interjects with the comment that every project needs to be developed, since they cannot stay in an unresolved form forever. They may be beautiful in their ambiguity, but people cannot live in that uncertainty. As designers you need to take a leap of faith, jump in, and develop your designs. The leap of faith is another way to express commitment based on a solid foundation. This is the recognition that the concept is valid, the initial choices are well founded, and the design can now be fully developed. To make a project real may be to define its physical reality. Often an undefined project that has undetermined edges and is comprised of abstract shapes is compelling to the imagination. The abstraction suggests a tremendous amount of potential, but constructing it physically makes it real and thus removes some of the mystery.

You will remember the discussion about Leon Battista Alberti and that a good definition of design is not only aesthetics, but the integration of everything necessary to make the project work in harmony. This means integrating all the technical, functional, and form qualities into a whole project – so that nothing is left out or imbalanced.[21] Basically, he states that a building is considered complete when it includes all the necessary parts. We are also reminded of Vitruvius' ideas about *Firmness*, *Commodity* and *Delight* – the things that define architecture and make it whole. So how can you be sure your projects contain everything they need? This can only happen through developing, defining, and describing the project. You have many models and drawings and have made decisions about the direction of the project, now you should develop it into a project that is presentable to your professor and potentially your clients. Developing a project means to refine the awkward, incongruous aspects and answer the unanswered questions. The questions that you will need to ask are different from those asked during conceptual stages. You should be sure to ask questions that pertain to refinement, such as what is the wall made of? Is the exit corridor too long? How do the mechanical systems work within the structure of the building? What is the feeling that your client will feel when occupying the space? If you are a beginning student the development of a project might include the craft required for refinement, meaning the clean precise resolution. In other words, this could mean refining the system or figuring out the method that reflects the fundamental issues of the assignment such as rhythm, pattern, focal point, or symmetry. It may also mean carrying the project to completion.

By now in your career as a student, you probably have realized that a project never feels finished, you can always add, fix, or refine. Maybe the project can be considered complete at the time of the deadline or on the due date, but most architects and designers feel that a project can always get better. Usually the completion happens when drawings go to the contractors or when clients are allowed to occupy the building. A project can be worked on forever, but it is your responsibility to bring it to sufficient completion. As students you probably have stayed up all night to finish a project for a deadline. It is understood that you feel you can keep working on it to improve it up until the last moment. Your professors do not advocate that you stay up all night to do this and it is not recommended. Instead you should plan ahead and articulate the boundaries that would make the project "finished." With these restrictions, you will know when it has reached a level of achievement or terminus and you can go home to sleep. Understanding what is expected of you (and the project) and what you expect of yourself, is the best way to avoid this dilemma. Managing your time is part of the process. Just as professionals plan work flow charts, you also should leave adequate time to develop ideas into physical form.

Design development is different than looking for conceptual beginnings, yet is equally important to the process and is an opportunity to make sure the construction, financial planning, and materials are as previously conceived. Development implies that the thing of concern is not green or immature, but ripened through time, external influences, and nourishment. As an analogy, a mature person is one who has grown to adulthood and has experience, knowledge, and growth sufficient to be refined.

Design development acts to portend the future. The refinement refers to the future building, where the architect or designer can begin to see the completed project. This development anticipates the solution similar to the workings of a divining rod. Historically, a divining rod is a forked stick that, held outstretched while walking across a site, is said to indicate the location of water, and thus the best place to drill a well. Most likely the holder of the divining rod was knowledgeable about the land features where water could be found (similar to abductive reasoning) but most importantly the user of the divining rod read the signs and pointed to the opportune site. It also indicated a view of the future in that *divining* is understood as "to foretell, or to know by inspiration, intuition or reflection."[22] Thus, when developing and presenting your design, you are looking to the future, defining what the project will look like and how it will function. Architects and designers are a bit like soothsayers, fortune-tellers, and magicians, because they envision future environments, and also show people with power and money what these environments will look like so that they can be constructed.

As discussed at the beginning of this book, the process of developing is not necessarily linear. Although theoreticians can describe the process of design, in reality it is seldom possible to follow definitive steps.[23] Each project is unique and must be approached according to its own character.

5.7 Men with divining rods search for treasure while others dig, in a sixteenth-century woodcut

Your design may seem to stop and start, various parts may be more difficult than others, and you may need to proceed and return to sticky issues. Geoffrey Broadbent writes about many methods that would constitute design process. Of many, it is helpful to think about your process in three parts; definition, solution, and critique. The first stage is to define the issue at hand in clear and concise terms (either verbally or visually). The second part is to arrive at a solution, and the third should critique the proposal. Once this is complete, you should start the process over to re-define, refine, and continually critique.

In most cases, to solve one thing opens opportunities to interpret and resolve other questions. You may find that you have been working under certain assumptions. If a new issue is brought to your attention, similar to a *deus ex machina* you may need to take a new tack. A *deus ex machina*, Latin for "god from the machine," represents a literary technique where, when the plot of a story becomes too complex and there is no way to resolve the situation, a totally different plotline is interjected. In the past, a new person or mechanical device would be interjected into the play (or dropped onto the stage) that would change the course of the narrative and determine the outcome.[24] When you cannot work something out, intervening with something totally different from outside your current thinking helps find a previously unconsidered solution, thus the phrase "thinking outside the box." You may have had several preliminary presentations about your design and have received direction concerning its validity from your professor or a visiting critic. Once this is done, you will certainly need to circle back to review what you have previously discovered or chosen, and you will need to allow the resolution of an issue to affect other issues. To detail a project is exactly what the word means – to get down to the details. Here you should accept the big picture and begin to see where specifics can be developed. The architectural theorist Marco Frascari writes about how the detail can be reflective of the entirety.[25] The detail carries the story of the concept and it conveys the meaning of the whole, such that themes of a *parti* can be shown in the approach of the smallest parts. Frascari speculates that buildings may be designed beginning with the details. In an example, the East Wing of the National Gallery in Washington, D.C., by I. M. Pei shows a similar relationship. The organization of the gallery is two adjacent triangles.

Pei uses this shape as a theme throughout the project, from the overall plan to the small air in-take covers under the main stair ways.

Detailing is part of developing. Details are the specific in contrast to the general big idea. Architects use the term *detailing* to mean the stages of looking at specifics, developing the finished aspects of a design. This usually means resolving the parts of the design that require working out. Details are the particulars, and for architects and designers this means attention to individual or minute parts of the design. For a project, this may require elaboration and clarification of sections of the design that are vague and unfinished. In your project, this phase may be answering the unanswered questions, or completing the project to its fullest extent. It can also mean finding out how things really work in a building, or its constructability. This may involve studying the joints and the connections that are important to having a project constructed, or getting to a finer level. The early vagueness of things such as connections need to be resolved with consideration for the qualities of materials, for example, how much of the joint is seen, how materials will sheer, and the sturdiness of the juncture. Through history, detailing has been of concern for architects. In different periods architectural theory has tried to resolve whether to cover difficult connections, how to finish rough edges, and when to intervene between the roughness of construction and the human inhabitant. For example, architects in the Modernist period, such as Mies van der Rohe, exposed structural elements, using them similar to ornament. Through history, architects have carefully covered rough places of intersection, such as where a wall meets the floor, with molding. Architectural theorists recognize that there is a difference between ornament and decoration. They both add to the look

5.8 Corner detail on TD Centre Towers,
Mies van der Rohe

of something through adornment, embellishment, or
enhancement, but where Mies van der Rohe stripped down
the extraneous to identify the structure as ornament, others
have added elements in a form of appliqué that could be
described as decoration.

Detailing usually involves moving from the general to the
specific. Where the general may be the large portions of a
building, the details are the smaller more specific items that
make the project appear finished. Part of the finish work is

covering imperfections. This usually involves moving from the outside to the inside, from the exterior of the building to the things that people interact with the most on the interior. It may also be described as moving from the large scale to the small scale. In this way, the construction must be concise, meaning succinct and precise.

SMOOTHING AND POLISHING

In the process of smoothing and polishing, you are inspecting your project to make sure everything is refined. Later in your education you will develop the project, which may include tasks such as making sure the column spacing of your structure is reasonable, the floor plans show correct dimensions rather than bubble diagrams, the sizes of mechanical rooms are accurately calculated, and checks have been made of the legalities of egress, in other words making sure that all the technical aspects are included. For early design students the process of refining might be a stage to ensure that your project reflects the concept or that your model is clean and self-explanatory. In either case, smoothing and polishing entails the final touches and refinements that are necessary to complete the project for presentation.

As an analogy, polishing is near the end of the preparation of a precious stone. Cutting and polishing a gem stone reveals its facets, where the process provides "reflecting surfaces creating ever-more-complex interrelationships between rays of light, which may be metaphorically compared to the ever-increasing complexity of literary or artistic structures ... the aim of cutting [the gem stone] is to bring it as close as possible to a perfection that its rough state prevents it from possessing."[26] To polish is to break down, or cut off the large rough parts and prepare the surface to be glossy. This usually means eliminating the coarseness that is large grained and

166   Defining

smoothing which is fine grained. The process makes the gem less rough and more precise as the facet edges are sharply defined. Like your project, the refining and polishing brings the project into focus, clarifying and defining it. Since you do not want others to misinterpret your intention, you should make sure the project is clear. If you are clear, then you can be reasonably assured that your future building will be constructed the way you envision it.

The Renaissance artist, sculptor, and architect, Michelangelo, wrote that he imagined the form of a figure in the mass of the rough stone. He allowed the shape of the uncut mass to suggest to him the form of the future sculpture. In this way, he described his process as cutting away the unwanted marble to reveal the form of the figure within. He claimed that he was only revealing the form that had been trapped in the stone.

In another analogy, this concept of smoothing and polishing may be akin to sharpening a knife. The whetstone wears off tiny bits of the blade to sharpen it. The action of sharpening eliminates the frayed edges to make the blade focused and free of extraneous elements. When we feel sharp, we are clear and intelligent in contrast to being dull or foggy. This analogy may be extended to question the difference between abstraction and precision in relationship to design definition and development. Abstraction suggests withdrawal and the idea that something does not have an independent existence. In other words, it is difficult to define and may exist only as an idea.[27] In contrast, making things more defined certainly makes them more technical and thus precise. Objects or ideas that are precise are those that are strictly interpreted and have defined boundaries. The smoothing and polishing of an architectural project is a matter of defining the technicalities. The craft of a project, for early year design students, is the precision or finished qualities. Craftsmanship means carefully cut edges (and clean glue joints) on your models, smudge-free drawings, accurate line weights, and completed shapes on your drawings either hand drawn or on the computer. Craft is the practice, the making, of a defined object, but it can also mean the deliberate precision of language, such as crafting a statement. This may be similar to deciding what something really is, the act of being very specific. This craft or precision is an act of finding the truth and also ensuring a complete project.

DESCRIBING

At times, during and after design development, you will need to make your project public. Your professor has spoken to you about your progress, your classmates have seen you working and an interim critique has revealed a good concept and some development, but you are probably wondering about the final presentation that will display the project's culmination, representing the outcome in its entirety. This may be similar to the analogy made by the fifteenth-century architect Filarete, who compares a building to a human being. The birth brings the baby forth into the world. Its presence shows its wholeness, although it is not fully mature yet. Prior to birth, the project is ripe with parturient possibility. It has potential and everyone can speculate about what it will look like. When born, the baby can be understood to have a wholeness, personality, and character. If able to be seen in its entirety, your project is complete enough to be described.

The words *describe* and *scribe* have similar roots. Something that can be described can be written about or explained.[28] In this way, a project reaches a point of clarity so that it can be stated explicitly. To describe something three-dimensionally includes understanding it enough to construct it. When you build a model of your concept, many questions arise as to how to build the representation. If too many questions remain unanswered then it is too difficult to build. Charles Eames writes that "Ideas are cheap. Always be passionate about ideas and communicating those ideas and discoveries to others in the things you make."[29] The act of making forces you to explain what the project will be. In another example, to successfully fabricate parts of a model with a laser cutter, you must be able to adequately describe the pieces digitally and build them in the computer program. If you cannot, then the computer will not talk to the laser cutter and communication breaks down.

Through refining the project, you can set boundaries to describe what the building will look like and how it performs. It is through fabrication or the action of making that you are able to stipulate parameters. As a brief note, the word *fabricate* also has connotations of falsity. To make

5.9 Land surveyor using odometer in the United States

something complete enough to view how it works may avoid any mistakes in the process. Thus, in another example, when architects write a list of specifications concerning products or materials used in a building, they are specifying how the particular object will look or perform. They are stating explicitly, and any substitutions need approval for eventual use. Describing then indicates that the project is complete enough for all its parts to be identified and appropriate enough to be made public.

When presenting his project in a review, Nathan spends much of his time explaining his project, what it should look like and how the spaces will function. Part way through his presentation, his professor stops him and says, "Nathan, you should not need to explain your project in such a lengthy way, instead your drawings should show your intent. The detail of the plans, sections, and elevations should present your project without you needing to say very much." What Nathan needs to realize is that when his presentation is complete the reviewers can read his drawings and should be able to understand the spaces, the materials, and construction elements. In your first years, it is important to remember that the critics have experienced similar projects in their education, they understand the principles and if your project is visually well described, they will comprehend what you are attempting to do. You may need to verbally explain your concept but if your drawings are clear you should not need to provide elaborate explanations. Nathan is reminded that in an earlier design review, the critics started talking about things unrelated to his project, and he asks himself whether his unclear drawings led the reviewers to misinterpret his project and discuss issues not pertinent to his intentions. He also thinks about a classmate's project that seemed so simple and clear but the critics did not spend much time discussing the outcome. Why does this happen? If a project is confusing and unresolved then reviewers are critical, but on the other hand, when projects are so clear they do not seem to appreciate the simple straightforward approach. Nathan is beginning to think that he and his classmates cannot win. Criticism will be discussed more thoroughly in chapter six, but a clear idea and a simplistic idea are two different things. It is always best to present your concepts clearly, while an overly simplistic concept will not spark enough interest to maintain a deep and thoughtful critique.

MAKING THE INVISIBLE VISIBLE

As Nathan discovered when presenting his project, he had an idea of a concept in his head but his drawings did not convey his intentions. The only way that you will be able to explain your concept accurately to your professors, critics, and fellow students is if you are able to bring your concept to life by making it visible. Your concepts and beliefs about the building are abstract and ambiguous until you can make them visible through their physical description.

There are two main types of images that are shown during a presentation: technical drawings like plans, sections, elevations, and details, and conceptual or artistic drawings such as sketches, diagrams, and renderings. Although many students probably think that professors ask for such a wide range of drawing for purely sadistic reasons, doing multiple drawings for a single building helps to work out any kinks in the design process, so that you can see the building as a whole. Both types of drawings should also help to reinforce the concept of the project, and should not be made simply because they were required. The more abstract drawings, like renderings, will show the audience the materiality, light quality, or spatial characteristics of a project, while the technical drawings will show how it can be constructed. Each type of drawing reinforces and enhances the others.

5.10 The power station sketch,
Antonio Sant'Elia

This Futurist drawing from the early 1900s by Antonio Sant'Elia shows a dynamic and imposing power plant. This drawing presents sufficient information to understand the type of building and its scale. As a less technical drawing, it appeals to the observer's emotions, indicates material qualities, and conveys the monumentality important to architects of the Futurist movement.

The section drawing of a mill represents an example of a technical drawing. Precise lines, description of the building's structure, and indications of how the mechanisms work sufficiently define what the building will be. These types of drawings adequately convey the spatial experience and construction details for most architects and laypeople to understand.

Although many studio projects are based on hypothetical sites, conditions, or problems, it is important to keep in mind that architecture is above all a physical art with tangible results. It may be helpful to think about

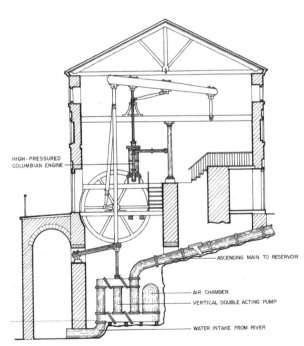

HIGH-PRESSURED COLUMBIAN ENGINE

ASCENDING MAIN TO RESERVOIR

AIR CHAMBER
VERTICAL DOUBLE ACTING PUMP

WATER INTAKE FROM RIVER

5.11 Cutaway view of the high pressured columbian engine water pumping system at Fairmount Water Works

the concept of *mimesis* when developing drawings for a presentation. Mimesis is "the representation of imitation of the real world in a work of art,"[30] and is a philosophical term that has been widely studied. Mimesis acts to bring certain aspects of everyday life into focus by exaggerating a simulated representation. The term *mime* has roots with the term *mimesis* because the performers use exaggerated gestures to present an object or situation that is not present.

It is through this type of simulated representation that Aristotle believed that meaning and emotion can be conveyed.[31] However, the exaggeration or stylization of reality is an important part of mimesis, because it "involves a framing of reality that announces that what is contained within the frame is not real."[32] As your professor may have told you when building models, you should not attempt to make your model hyper realistic, because this will simply make it apparent that the model is not real. Instead, an exaggeration or stylization of real life materials will be much more effective at conveying your original intent. Emphasizing the parts of your project that are more important helps to ensure that everyone understands what you are trying to accomplish.

Alison has been working hard on her model of a small hiking pavilion. The natural setting is a dominant feature in the program for the project and also part of her conceptual thinking. The evening before the project is due, she decides to paint the entire site that would be grass, a green hue. On the day of the presentation, her professor is quite surprised at the green paint, and he says, "Do you know why most architects use neutral colors and abstract landscape features to model their projects? This is because, although grass is certainly green, when you paint it a vivid green, it is so realistic that it appears unreal.

In other words, the bright green brings the project into a reality of the paint and the illusion of the project is lost. Models are representations and they help us to use our imaginations to project what the future of the building will look like. The paint is a distraction and because it is paint it changes the scale and we are confused about the paint as grass. Another reason to use neutral colors (and abstract forms for trees), is that you do not want to distract attention from your proposed building. Models, in most cases, are used primarily to show form and spatial relationships so that making miniature bricks for your small scale models is unnecessary." The professor sighs and adds, "What I am saying may not be entirely true since next year you will be making larger models of a wall section where we will expect you to replicate materials and connections." It is not necessarily wise to think about replicating building materials since plaster does not really act like concrete, but again plaster may be a poured material that can provide the abstract idea. Again, many of the decisions as to what materials to use depend upon the scale of the model, your focus and your intention.

In the stage of design when describing and defining your project, you must realize that the future building cannot be constructed full-scale in these early stages of design development. Even though architects often mock-up parts of their designs such as wall sections, they must be able to envision the building though drawing conventions such as plans, sections, elevations, perspectives, and also models. And of course, it is important to teach clients to read these abstractions or provide realistic renderings to assist them to imagine the building.

An issue that you might encounter when presenting your drawings is that a single image can be interpreted in a wide variety of ways, despite your original intention.

As Jacques Aumont wrote in his text, *The Image*, "each image has, in effect, a life of its own,"[33] and you may not always have the opportunity to explain your image or resulting building. The faculty members reviewing your project might ask you not to speak, hoping to let your representations tell the story of your project. As Juhani Pallasmaa writes in *The Embodied Image*, "we grasp the entity, the 'anatomy' and the meaning of an image before we are able to identify its details, or understand it intellectually."[34]

Architectural images are promises and invitations[35] for interpretation due to their highly metaphorical nature, and for the fact that they refer to the future. As mentioned earlier, architecture portends the future by interpreting the signs, and it is through architectural images that these future conditions are represented. Whether or not your idea of the future, or your concept for how people inhabit the world, is understood by others is highly dependent on your final images, and the way that you present them.

The ability to define, refine, and describe your designs is critical to assess their qualities. In a similar way, it is important for your presentations to be clear so that others can evaluate and criticize your work.

Endnotes

1. The *Compact Edition of the Oxford English Dictionary* (Oxford: Oxford University Press, 1971), s.v. "definition."
2. *Oxford English Dictionary*, s.v. "designing."
3. John William Miller, *The Definition of a Thing* (New York: W.W. Norton and Co., 1980), 43, 50, 159.
4. Peter A. Angeles, *Dictionary of Philosophy* (New York: Barnes and Noble Books, 1981), 55–59.
5. Miller, *The Definition of a Thing*, 42, 50.
6. See Jean Baudrillard, *Simulations*, trans. Paul Foss, Paul Patton, and Philip Beitchman (New York: Semiotext(e), 1983).
7. Benjamin Franklin Wilson III, *The Parthenon of Pericles and its Reproduction in America* (Nashville: Parthenon Press, 1937), 33.
8. Ibid.
9. See George Hershey, *The Lost Meaning of Classical Architecture* (Cambridge, MA: MIT Press, 1988).
10. *Oxford English Dictionary*, s.v. "simulacrum."
11. See Richard Kearney, *The Wake of the Imagination* (Minneapolis: University of Minnesota Press, 1988).
12. See Leon Battista Alberti, *On the Art of Building in Ten Books*, trans. Joseph Rykwert, Neil Leach, and Robert Tavernor (Cambridge, MA: MIT Press, 1988).
13. *Oxford English Dictionary*, s.v. "design."
14. Moshe Barasch, *Theories of Art from Plato to Winckelman* (New York: New York University Press 1985), 217–219. Also see Francis Ames-Lewis and Joanne Wright, *Drawings in the Italian Renaissance Workshop* (London: Victoria and Albert Museum, 1983) and Stephen Parcell, *Four Historical Definitions of Architecture* (Montreal: McGill-Queen's University Press, 2012).
15. Barasch, *Theories of Art from Plato to Winckelman*, 218–219.
16. Cited by James Smith Pierce, "Architectural Drawings and the Intent of the Architect," *Art Journal* 27 (1967), 57–58.
17. Anthony Antoniades, *Architecture and Allied Design* (Dubuque and Toronto: Kendall/Hunt Publishing Company, 1980), 46.
18. *Oxford English Dictionary*, s.v. "clarity."
19. Francis D. K. Ching, *Form, Space, and Order* (Hoboken: John Wiley & Sons, 2007), 415.
20. Thomas Bulfinch, *The Age of Fable* (New York: The Heritage Press, 1942), 160; Penelope Doob, *The Idea of the Labyrinth* (Ithaca: Cornell University Press, 1990), 160; and Alberto Perez-Gomez "The Myth of Daedalus," *A.A. Files* 10 (1985), 49–50.
21. Alberti, *On the Art of Building in Ten Books*, 156.
22. A divining rod takes its name from *divine*. According to the *Oxford English Dictionary* the etymology of the word *divine* comes not only from the Latin *divinus*, pertaining to a deity, but also from the Latin *divinare*, to foretell or predict.
23. See Geoffrey Broadbent, *Design in Architecture* (Chichester, New York, Brisbane, Toronto: John Wiley & Sons, 1973).
24. *Oxford English Dictionary*, s.v. "deus ex machina."
25. See Marco Frascari, "The Tell the Tale Detail," in *Via 7: The Building of Architecture*, eds. Paula Behrens and Anthony Fisher (Cambridge, MA: The MIT Press, 1984) 23–37.
26. Judith Robinson-Valéry, "The 'Rough' and the 'Polished'," *Yale French Studies* 89 (1996): 60.
27. *Oxford English Dictionary*, s.v. "abstraction."
28. *Oxford English Dictionary*, s.v. "describe."
29. "iz quotes," last modified 2014, accessed March 8, 2014, http://izquotes.com/quote/55046.
30. *Oxford English Dictionary*, s.v. "mimesis."
31. S. H. Butcher (trans.), *Aristotle's Theory of Poetry and Fine Art* (New York: Dover Publications, 1951), 121–123.
32. Michael Davis, *Poetry of Philosophy* (South Bend, IN: St. Augustine's Press, 1993), 3.
33. Jacques Aumont, *The Image* (London: British Film Institute, 1997), 199.
34. Juhani Pallasmaa, *The Embodied Image; Imitation and Imagery in Architecture* (Chichester, UK: John Wiley and Son, 2011), 43.
35. Ibid., 123.

Assessing

Chapter 6

Criticism is a misconception:
we must read not to understand
others but to understand
ourselves.

Emile M. Cioran

Criticism can be useful in helping you to assess the problems with your design. As has been mentioned earlier, criticism can offer you assistance in stepping away to look at your project as others see it. It is difficult to be objective and giving yourself distance from a project can present you with a fresh perspective. The purpose of the design review process is to provide students and professionals with input into the design solution for a specific project. Someone who has not been part of the design process can provide critical distance. Designers are often too close to the process, and because they are so focused on the chosen solution they cannot see the faults in the design.[1] For you as a student, recognizing the things that are positive or negative about your project becomes more distinct through criticism, and can be brought to the surface for consideration.

Criticism is an important aspect of architecture and design education, but it is also necessary in the professional lives of practitioners. Architects are constantly in competition with their peers for building contracts. Each building constructed is an advertisement for the next project, and every architect understands that personal recommendations and professional contacts influence the ability to obtain new projects. Architectural societies such as the American Institute of Architects, Royal Architectural Institute of Canada, Australian Institute of Architects, and the Royal Institute of British Architects celebrate excellence locally and nationally with building awards. Receiving awards from your peers can contribute to greater exposure for contracts. As with art, theater, and music criticism, architecture critics review projects for professional, academic, and public forums. Currently, however, most large newspapers or professional journals do not regularly publish critical reviews of new buildings.

Various forms of criticism occur throughout the process of building. Some cities and communities require design review of public buildings. Certainly, zoning boards approve architectural projects before they are constructed. The design process also has checks and balances, since there are many participants in the construction of a building such as consultants, contractors, and clients. More common in Europe than North America, many contracts are awarded through competition. Some competitions are open, and receive entries from around the world. These competitions are usually judged by prominent architects who choose the best projects through elimination, usually over a period of a few days. Other competitions are invited and solicit proposals from appropriate professional firms depending on the scope of the construction, often called a request for proposal.

The review process in schools is also competitive. Your projects may be evaluated against other projects completed in a studio or your grades may be based solely on the quality of the project. Many

6.1 Students critique each other's work in this graphic design class

students feel intense competition to produce the best project in the studio and this is understandable. Recently, educational institutions have recognized the collaborative nature of the architectural profession and attempted to replicate this in schools. You may be assigned group projects; however, it is hard for professors to evaluate each student within the group, so you will also be completing many designs individually. Criticism and assessment are part of the environment and your experiences in school educate you to understand criticism from others and learn to develop a critical attitude.

Sam and James walk by the third year critique spaces and hear several faculty members and guest practitioners reviewing final projects. They are shocked that the critics are so negative and do not seem to like any of the projects. Why aren't the students upset about the comments? How difficult it must be to defend your project and how hard it must be to explain all the thinking that went into designing it. Sam and James know that their first review is coming up in two weeks and they do not know what to expect. Called either a design jury, studio review, project review, or critique (crit), the act of providing feedback to students concerning their design projects is vital to learning architectural design.

As you know by now, architecture and design students are afforded a unique educational experience in the design studio. Considering a one-on-one relationship with their studio instructor, small classes, and a 24/7 environment, this education is uniquely personal and a design jury is an aspect of this intimate education. In a critique, faculty members and guest critics spend time listening to students present their projects and subsequently the jury gives specific and targeted comments about each student's project. This is far different than large lecture classes that depend upon Scantron exams for assessment. In most cases, you receive weekly personal critiques preparing you for interim and final reviews. Your studio professors most likely talk about the requirements for the project regularly to identify the strong points or problems with your design and advise you on next steps to improve your projects. Typically, not wanting to design your project for you, your professors may give you substantial autonomy while informing you of problems that need to be resolved. Often this critique is subtle and you should be listening for it because it is easy to ignore comments that you do not want to hear or would mean extra effort in redesign. To make criticism less intimidating, often interim reviews are more informal or in a group setting. Although there are variations on the structure of design reviews, this environment reflects the long tradition of criticism in the arts and humanities, such as movie, theater, and music.

Criticism emerges from the French *critique*, concerning judgment or decision. To effectively criticize something requires knowledge or a foundation of what is better than something else. If people do not have wide experiences they do not have the knowledge necessary for comparison.

For example, judges have extreme knowledge of the law, and art critics must be very knowledgeable of aesthetics and its history. The French philosopher Michel Foucault influenced the use of the word *critique* rather than criticism.[2] Critique implied greater depth of meaning and consideration. Foucault also equated critique with the judgment of discourse and this evaluation was understood as more structured. He introduces the skeptical questioning of authority and the critique that attempts to find what is true.

Architectural and design crits have roots in both historic guilds and the academic realm. In the academic tradition dating back to the ancient Greeks, scholars who wished to become doctors or masters were required to defend their thesis work through a series of public lectures and debates.[3] During the Middle Ages, when apprentices in a guild sought to become journeymen, they were asked to produce and present an example of their work to the masters. The masters examined the work and asked the apprentice a series of probing questions about the field. The apprentices who passed this exam

6.2 Meeting of doctors at the University of Paris

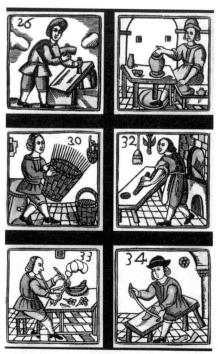

6.3 Tiles with medieval representations of six Trade Union trades

advanced to journeyman status, allowing them to undertake freelance projects.[4]

The jury system in design education emerged from the École des Beaux Arts in Paris. A master, who was usually also a practitioner, led each group of students in a studio (*atelier*). Through an apprentice type exchange, each student developed an outline or sketch, called an *esquisse*, into a project.[5] At the time a project was due, a cart was wheeled through the studio to collect the drawings. As you can imagine there was a rush to finish the last details to ensure the drawings were included on the cart.[6] These drawings were then hung on the walls of a jury room for faculty members to evaluate. Originally the jury, discussing the students' projects, occurred behind closed doors so that students would not be able to hear faculty members' comments.[7] As another educational model, the Bauhaus tradition founded in Germany was based in a studio culture of making and thus presented an added dimension to the *atelier* model. This type of studio encompassed all the arts and was concerned with fabrication and hands-on experience. Early architects in North America who had been trained at the École des Beaux Arts or the Bauhaus schools brought these traditions to universities in the New World.[8] The traditions of art criticism may

6.4 Bauhaus Dessau main building from the south

have also influenced the emphasis on juries and design reviews. In any case, seeking opinions of educators and professionals provides a different perspective for you as you learn about design. Design is very subjective because there are so many variables and alternatives, so an opportunity to hear from those with experience can be valuable.

Let us first define a studio project review, the process, and the players. Nearly every architecture student has at some time presented in a crit and certainly most remember these reviews as a challenging experience. What exactly is an architectural crit? The word *crit* is short for criticism, or critique, and emerges from the words *decide* or *judge*.[9] Other versions of the word show an interesting relationship between *critical* and *crisis*, since in medicine *critical* is crucial or imminent, where the term *criticality* suggest accuracy and precision.[10] In a crit, students present their design projects to their instructor and sometimes invited critics, often with an audience of students and guests. A design review is usually scheduled after your project is complete, although it may also take place when your project is in the process of development as a preliminary or interim review. Generally you display and explain your project in front of the critics. Once you present your project the critics will typically offer their opinions concerning your work. Good criticism will ideally be clear, concise, and to the point. It could be candid, positive, negative, or speculative. The critics will usually frame their comments in such a way so you understand and can act on what is said. It is always useful to have a fellow student take notes about what the critics tell you during your crit since crits can be quite stressful, and you are unlikely to remember all that you have been told.

6.5 Atelier de Gainier

Experts evaluate your project based on the program, site, and criteria of appropriateness in relationship to context, architectural principles, and precedent, to name a few. It is important to recognize that a critique is based on criteria, and critics will want to know what you are trying to accomplish. In other words, you lay the foundation (your set of parameters by identifying a concept) and your solution (the building) against the parameters of the project. In many cases, the critics are not given boundaries to limit their comments; they will voice opinions on any or all of your decisions. They will of course be given the project statement and most often will use that to focus their criticism. To give their comments perspective and to help you understand, they often add into this discussion their knowledge of precedent using examples from their education and experience. They are able to use this comparative background to form opinions about your project. They call upon projects that they have seen and experienced, and employ their understanding of architectural history, theory, and technology. These critics comment on successful aspects of your decisions and also less successful decisions, usually providing both positive and negative comments and, more importantly, giving you suggestions about what you can do to improve. The most successful design reviews are treated as a dialogue to help you learn.

Criticism varies depending upon your level in school and the parameters of the project. You may ask why criticism happens so late in the process, after the projects are finished. You may also wonder how students can receive criticism when they have such limited knowledge of the field. When Sam and James stop at the back of the review, they ask the upper year students these questions. A fourth year student responds by saying, "Usually a crit happens when a project is completed enough to be able to be criticized. If critics review a project too early, it is full of potential and not yet resolved. This makes it hard for the critics to fully understand the resolution of intention and thus it is difficult to achieve a complete and useful discussion. This is why the formal reviews occur at the end of each semester, since the project needs to be complete enough for thoughtful criticism. The focus of the review changes depending upon your year in school. As you may notice the projects become more complex each semester, reflecting your stage in the program and the criticism reflects the level of complexity. The repetition, doing a project and hearing external criticism, of the process helps you learn. If you experience the process only once, you do not have the opportunity to improve or learn from mistakes. Remember that your project will never be perfect and the reviewers will always provide some negative criticism. There is always room for improvement and even if you have a good project they will always try to challenge you with the next level of thinking."

Because you are emotionally attached to your project, and you have been staying up all night finishing the presentation, criticism may seem harsher than you might expect. Again, you must remember that the reviewers are commenting on your project, not on you as a person. This process tends to be highly emotional and is heightened further by your stress level. Kathryn Anthony in her book *Design Juries on Trial* writes about strategies to deal with this stress, and certainly familiarity with the practice makes you less emotionally sensitive to the criticism.[11] Adequately preparing for your presentation is part of this strategy. Organizing your thoughts by writing notes that clearly identify your concept and main points can help you be clear in this presentation. Remember that the critics will base their criticism on what you say in comparison to what you present. In other words, what you state as your priorities and the focus of your drawings, renderings, and models will frame their comments. They will carefully listen to your concepts and decisions, and evaluate them against the project that you display. So it is important to be both concise and precise – if you say too much the discussion could easily get off topic to something you were not really considering. However, if you say too little they may not fully understand what you are trying to accomplish.

Criticism has several important dimensions. First, it is through your own criticism of your work that you will need to be able to step back and ask yourself if the work is really performing as needed. Many beginning students get far too close to their own work to see the flaws that need to be fixed. Second, is the peer-review you receive from your fellow students. This can be useful because your fellow students are often working on the same project and are well aware of the problems involved. Often your friends will find it difficult to criticize your work because they may want to remain your friend. You can make them understand that their criticism of your project is welcome and will not be taken personally. Third, to review the progress of your project your instructor, or other professors, will visit your desk in the studio. When the project is in process, your professors cannot be as thorough in their comments because they cannot see the final outcome. Obviously, your instructors cannot fully comprehend what you are visualizing the project will look like when it is finished. The more you have completed to show them, whether it be models or drawings, the more assistance they can provide to you. For this type of studio review, it can be useful to ask the instructor some direct questions about the problems you are encountering. This can save time, help the criticism be more targeted, and allow your process to move forward.

STEPPING AWAY

Linda was confident going into her design review. She had been working really hard over the semester on her project and felt it was one of the best in the studio. After presenting, however, the critics noted issues with details that she thought were great. They didn't seem to get her project at all. Seeing Linda's face start to fall, one of the critics spoke up. "I think you've been living in the Monkey House," he said. "When you go to the zoo and first enter the Monkey House, you think to yourself 'This place stinks!' But after you've been there for a few minutes, it doesn't seem so bad, and after an hour you don't notice anything at all."

After spending weeks working on a project, you may find it difficult to be unbiased. You have been working every day figuring out the right concept, how to organize circulation, and what drawings to include in your presentation, and you become overly attached to the project and have a hard time critiquing it. This is why it is extremely important to take a little time away from the project at various points in the process to be able to come back to it with fresh eyes. While you may not always have the luxury of a lot of time between various stages of design and the project hand-in or the critique, step away from the computer and take a walk, talk to your roommate, or simply take a shower to get out and away from the Monkey House.

One benefit of stepping away from your project is that you can then present the project with detachment. The act of presenting your project forces you to make your intention clear and concise, in such a way that a large number of people can understand it. Remember that while your professor and classmates may have seen your project a number of times before in a desk crit or interim presentations, often the critics arrive with only a basic understanding of the project parameters. What you intend and what is perceived may be very different, so it is important to look at your project without emotional investment. Also, remember that the critics are desperately trying to think of things to say that will help you in the ten minutes or so of your presentation. You can help them by directing them to your primary decisions.

Much like an Impressionist painting, you need to step back to consider the whole picture instead of just the individual brushstrokes. Ask yourself if your project met all the criteria required of the project. Were you able to complete everything that you wanted to? If you were seeing your project for the first time, how would you critique it? It might even be helpful to present your project to a friend or family member before the final critique to see if they understand your intention and if they have any comments on the project. Above all, try to put some distance between yourself and your project.

Stepping away from your project is both important and difficult. You have spent many weeks with your design and you are emotionally invested in the solution, thus it is difficult to be self-critical since you have justified the design at every decision point. Obtaining external criticism helps you balance your solution with input from others. As mentioned previously, the Renaissance architect Filarete compared the design of a building to a human baby. He wrote that the idea can be likened to the conception, a gestation period is very much akin to design development and construction, and the birth of the child is similar to presentation stages.[12] When the child is born, it is visible to the world and all the aunts and uncles visit to see this newborn. Of course, the infant does not yet have a personality, but these relatives can judge the baby on what they see. They count the fingers and toes to assess its completeness and compare the child to others in the family, saying she looks like her mother did at that age and her eyes are the color of Aunt Helen's. Your project may be like this baby, since the critics can judge what you produced from the concept to the details.

The important thing is not to take critique personally. Although many critics may seem harsh, the final critique is above all a learning experience. You have the ability to learn from your own mistakes, and those of your classmates, and correct them for the next project. Also remember that not all critics come to the same conclusion about a project; some of the most interesting projects are those that can be debated. One critic may love your project while another may hate it; architecture can be incredibly subjective. But hearing the discussion gives you perspective and can be an opportunity to understand more about how your project is perceived. This conversation can also assist you to learn from the critics' experience with design.

Architectural firms use different techniques of self-criticism in an effort to step away and be objective. Some firms may bring in visitors or colleagues to review projects while they are in process. Large architecture firms divide the projects in their offices into teams and the teams may critique each other. This can be particularly effective since all involved understand the goals of the firm and it is to their advantage to provide honest and collegial feedback. Architectural firms, especially those involved with public projects, often solicit opinions from the community at large. This may involve presenting at community forums or utilizing social media for commentary. Most architectural practices use the periodic dialogue with their clients to gain valuable input throughout the process. Meetings with the future users of a building allow architects to continually reassess and adjust their designs. Clients can then become more specific about their needs and desires, and subsequently architects can respond to their requests. This dialogue attempts to gain optimal quality for the finished building.

IDENTIFYING STRENGTHS AND WEAKNESSES

It is typically considered that humans are inherently less than perfect, and so are the things that they produce. Your design reviews will most likely include a combination of positive comments and things that you can do to improve. If you can assume that criticism will make your projects better, you can see the exercise as a learning experience. It is the nature of humans, traditionally and historically, to strive for perfection. Even criticism that is laid against a good project will help you learn and improve.

Sarah and Elena have been discussing a studio review and are surprised that it seemed the critics spent a lot of time discussing the theory and details of an upper year student's project. They relay that the project received an "A" for a grade and the whole committee admitted that the project was very successful. Why did it feel like the critics were tearing apart the project with so much discussion? In this case, because the project was good the critics could talk about the well-developed theories and how the project raised interesting questions.

When reviewing a poor project, there is little opportunity for dialogue since the ideas are often superficial and underdeveloped. In the case of a project that is underdeveloped or begins with a poor premise, there is little intellectual stimulus to spark a conversation. This may be reflected in the number of comments that a student receives. With a poor project, the critics may find it harder to give constructive criticism or tell the student how to proceed. Since the critics are all interested in the education of future architects and designers, they try to utilize the critique as an educational tool. Sometimes they may speak less about what you have completed and more about how to move forward, how you can learn from the project or how to develop it even further. They also may see a studio critique as an opportunity to introduce the class to theoretical positions or new technologies, materials, or techniques that the students have not experienced yet. It may sound as if they are getting off-topic, but instead they see a good time and place to inject relevant and related material into a conversation. Good critics all want the next generation of professionals to excel and achieve things greater than they were able to. With this in mind, the best critics will challenge your thinking and try to expand your perceptions. They will not feel competitive with you but instead direct and encourage your explorations. They should not impose their solutions but rather react to your approach and concentrate on how to assist you to reach your goals. Since professors and critics all have different teaching styles, an adage may describe the types you may encounter: *the guide on the side or the sage on the stage.*

The *guide on the side* describes an instructor who helps students discover knowledge and steers their development. This professor is not necessarily the teacher that is lecturing constantly but one who continually poses thoughtful questions to help you find your own direction. These professors often do not dictate, but instead encourage interactive learning. Just as a guide points the way, a guide on the side points out interesting things to consider and keeps you from getting lost. This faculty member may give you numerous options to consider or suggest interesting precedent for you to study. In this manner, they are using the method of teaching through dialogue. You might feel frustrated that this type of instructor is not giving you a straight answer, or is continually elusive. Although you may wish to receive a definitive answer, in the long run the instructor who helps you to arrive at your own conclusions may serve you best.

The *sage on the stage* is a professor or critic with extensive knowledge or professional experience who speaks well and presents with captivating and convincing information. These people could be labeled as experts expounding wisdom. They may excel in the presentation of information but not be able to help you think through your beliefs. It is important to listen to such a faculty member, with a definitive opinion, as they may assist you to clarify your own beliefs. Either you find that you agree, and this assists you to solidify your position, or you understand better as to why you disagree. Be aware that you may be tempted to copy their style of architecture or assume their theories without question. This may lead to imitation without understanding, a tenuous position for you as a student. Sometimes the *sage on the stage* is less approachable and it is difficult to receive individual attention because they are continually surrounded by others seeking attention. This may seem the case, but often this type of instructor has a tremendous amount of experience and their teachings will provide thoughtful insight.

Obviously you will run across various teachers with quite different teaching styles. You will most likely gravitate to those who you feel can help you the most, and who you choose may change depending upon the stage of your education. As mentioned earlier, studio education is certainly one-on-one and provides personal attention. This model is not unlike the Socratic

6.6 Socrates teaching Perikles

method where studio critique is a form of inquiry and debate.[13] This dialogue of questions and answers intends to teach critical thinking, and is usually meant to help students look at a subject from many perspectives.

A similar educational technique is a *dialectical* method that is based on oppositional discussion. This method examines an opinion to find the truth, usually investigated through discussion.[14] The German philosopher, Georg Wilhelm Friedrich Hegel, writes about a critical method that is often useful to designers, *thesis*, *antithesis*, and *synthesis*. Identifying a thesis (a proposition) sets the stage to look at the opposite position, the antithesis. This opposing view is similar to finding the faults and gives you an alternative perspective. The synthesis brings the two sides together and helps you to reconcile the conflict and get closer to a truth.[15] In your case, the truth may be as good a solution to your project assignment as possible. Most of your professors will engage in a *Teacher/Scholar* method where they heighten the level of learning by bringing their own research into the classroom.[16]

The educational psychologist, Donald Schön, calls a feedback learning process of critique, reflection in action. In his book, *The Reflective Practitioner: How Professionals Think in Action*, he describes reflective practice as the capacity to reflect upon your actions (what you have experienced) so that you can continuously learn from your experiences and mistakes.[17] Based on the teachings of John Dewey, Schön feels that this ability to learn from reflection is an important tool in practice-based professional learning. In other words, he is advocating for learning from one's own personal and professional experiences rather than traditional formal settings such as lectures. These two thinkers understand the knowledge that can be obtained through the recognition and alteration of something that did not work, in actuality learning by doing. Remember that people learn by hearing and seeing, but the insight necessary to synthesize that knowledge into an action become internalized and remembered.

Identifying the strengths and weaknesses of what you have done is important to your development as a designer, whether you find out from someone else or discover this fact on your own. You should not be afraid to ask yourself what you did wrong, and what you can do better next time. This can help you circle back and learn from what you have completed. The project may need extensive revision, or may only require minor alterations. You might, after a good night's sleep, revisit the critics' comments to decide how far back you need to go in your process to address their concerns.

The most successful architects are able to be self-critical. They continually question decisions without letting this questioning retard the progress of the project. For example, some firms, recognizing the importance of global sustainability, will constantly compare what they design to accepted energy standards.

QUESTIONING THE CONCEPT

The first year crit had been on for several hours when John presented his project. The three invited critics examined John's work and commented that although the idea behind the project was very interesting, the drawings and model were inconsistent with his concept and very poorly crafted. One critic said, "This is an example of a great idea that was presented poorly and because of this it is unlikely that it would be built." Another critic continued, "That in many ways is much worse than a bad idea presented poorly which shouldn't be built for good reason." The third critic smiled at this and said, "Good ideas in architecture have the potential to improve the lives of the people of the world therefore they should be presented clearly and persuasively. Let me give you an historical example of this. Fillipo Brunelleschi's entry for the 1418 competition

6.7 The dome of the Florence cathedral

to build the new dome for the Florence cathedral offers us an example of a good idea presented well. At first Brunelleschi presented his idea to the committee by standing an egg upright, breaking its bottom. While this demonstration proved interesting, the committee asked for more proof and this was provided in the form of an ingenious wood and brick model.[18] This model clearly demonstrated how the proposed revolutionary dome could be built using internal stone and iron chains to hold its shape like a barrel. The committee was eventually convinced by this persuasive demonstration and his idea for the dome was built. It is generally believed that the invention of Brunelleschi's dome was an important foundation of the Renaissance."

The third critic continued, "But don't forget that a bad idea can be presented very persuasively. Let me tell you about Albert Speer. Speer, who was well known as Hitler's architect, stated that he wasn't interested in politics as a young man but became swept up in the popularity of the Nazi Party in the 1930s. Here he gained the interest of Hitler and was offered many design commissions. One of Speer's first commissions was the design of the Nuremberg parade grounds, a site for enormous Nazi rallies. Speer

Assessing

recommended that most events on the site be held at night and then surrounded the grounds with 130 anti-aircraft searchlights. This created a 'cathedral of light' which Speer described as his most beautiful work.[19] This demonstration was incredibly powerful, influencing many to join the party. However, while many agree that this was a fine piece of architecture, most also believe that the Nazi philosophy was a very bad idea. At the end of the war, Speer was sentenced to twenty years imprisonment for his support of the Nazi Party. I have told you the story of Brunelleschi and Speer for a reason. While each were able to create very interesting projects, one was more ethical than the other. Few today would argue about Albert Speer's ethical problems. Being ethical, being able to decide what is good or bad, is your moral duty and obligation as a professional."

As a student and future practitioner, it is important to remember that the ethical qualities of your concepts, reflecting your beliefs, are your responsibility and

6.8 Mass assemblage of political leaders on the searchlight-illuminated Zeppelin field, Nuremberg

ultimately establish your reputation. Equally important is how you define, describe, and represent environments for your clients. Models, drawings, and particularly renderings can be extremely compelling. They can convince to the point of seduction. Recognizing the power of images can assist in making decisions as you prepare for

6.9 The Drawbridge, plate VII from
the series *Carceri d'Invenzione*

Assessing

presentations. The beautiful, experiential, and atmospheric drawings by architects such as Lebbeus Woods, Massimo Scolari, Aldo Rossi, and Giovanni Battista Piranesi may help you realize the influence images can have to persuade conceptual ideas.

This etching by Giovanni Battista Piranesi presents an example of a persuasive image. Piranesi (1720–1778) was an engraver of Roman antiquities. His series of scenes of presumably underground spaces is called *Carceri*, which could be translated as prison. The location appears to be a large interior underground space that evokes decay and oppression. On closer inspection many inconsistencies and ambiguities can be observed. The light seems to be omnipresent, not necessarily emanating from one direction. The representation of space is confusing since he seems to mix foreground and background. In fact, Piranesi used numerous perspective points to make the observer feel off balance, lost in continuous space. Repeated vertical railings and the layered horizontal walkways reinforce the fragmented uncertainty of the space. The architectural theorist Manfredo Tafuri suggests that this is purposeful on the part of Piranesi in order to demonstrate a view of political repression.[20] Piranesi used the inconsistencies and incorrect perspective of the *Carceri* to present a conceptual truth and persuade the observer.

No matter how seductive the drawings, the essence of your concepts should show prominently in your presentation. Even the faulty ideology of Albert Speer's light palace was inspirational to those who witnessed it. In questioning your concepts you should utilize criticism to assess if you are on the right track. The criticism will hopefully separate your idea from your presentation, although the eye candy of a beautiful presentation can make it more difficult for critics. The act of criticism gives you feedback to validate your decisions. Seeing the project finished, stepping away for perspective, and hearing criticism allow you to test your concepts. Before the review of your project by external critics, you should compare your concept to what you plan to say and what you have presented in the form of models and drawings. These two should match, since the critics will certainly be comparing them. To assure there is a logical relationship between your conceptual thinking and the final project, it may be wise to either think about presentation while you are designing or employ the act of presenting to help you in your design process. You may remember that chapter three discussed using various media to think through issues. It is never a good idea to leave choosing a presentation technique to the last minute. It is far better to think ahead and continue to develop your project as you prepare presentation drawings.

After a preliminary critique there is time to reassess your concept and to continue the development of the project. You can carefully revisit your concept once you have heard comments and analyzed them with your crit buddy. You can also use the progressive development of the project to help you work out unresolved concerns that were brought to light by the criticism. What should you change? How much should you change? And what changes can you make in the time before the project is finally due without completely starting over? Sometimes students cannot distance themselves enough to recognize the problems and cannot give up a poor idea. This ability to be critical and cut your losses takes experience. Most architects have learned when to take a critical turn and abandon a poor concept. Remember, you are young and if an idea is not working for this project you can save it for another project.

REASSESSING

Final critiques are most often at the end of the term and subsequently mark the end of a project. If you received negative criticism, you may be discouraged and want to put your project away and forget about it. But

6.10 Architecture students from Ryerson University during a trip to Turkey

reassessing your project after a critique not only helps you to make better decisions in the future, but also helps to create a portfolio piece that you can be proud of.

After a critique, you should ask yourself if you communicated your thoughts well, and if you received negative comments, was this because the critics misunderstood? Were they confused about your concept? Were your drawings unclear? You should also consider their comments carefully – maybe you disagree with them. Remember they are desperately trying to think of something intelligent to say about each project (in the span of 10 minutes) that will impress their fellow critics and also help you become a better designer. This is a tall order. With that said, could they have given you poor comments? Undoubtedly you will experience this at least once in your time at school. You should logically ask yourself if you are being stubborn, or if you really did not get helpful criticism. Critics are not perfect and certainly do not get it right every time. They may also be from a different generation, educated within an earlier paradigm, be overly influenced by what is fashionable or not fashionable, expound a different philosophy or once in practice may be concentrating on the overly practical aspects of architectural design. When do you ignore criticism? In the end it is your project and you need to assess their assessment in relationship to your project and your concept. There are of course, stories of famous architects who were too radical while they were in school and were continually evaluated negatively by more conservative critics. Although your instructors try to invite the professionals best able to be helpful in your process this is not always possible. On the other hand, these critics are experts and you should take their criticism seriously. Your school has a reputation to uphold, along with accreditation criteria, so you can be reasonably assured that the comments are valid and meant to be helpful, and you should consider them carefully. Architectural educators are trying to help their students comprehend the world in a new manner, and to question the current state of architecture. It is critical to trust in the experience and insight that your professors provide. Again, try to be logical and detached when you evaluate which comments to follow.

You may recall that images can be used for recording information, design discovery, and visualizing, but they can also be utilized for testing and evaluation. You have tested the waters, so to speak. You tried an approach and have received criticism about that direction. This is good. Now you can make more informed decisions as you move forward. If you and your classmates did not receive any comments you would be concerned, wondering if your projects were good. Remember this is a learning process and if you analyze the criticism you can learn from your mistakes.

Reassessing can come at one of two major points in your project, either after an interim critique or a final critique. It is important to note that while many students may feel that the final critique is the most important, it is actually the interim critique that can provide the most help. At an interim critique, you are most likely about halfway towards the completion of your project, and while some comments may feel harsh, they allow for your initial ideas to be assessed without having taken them too far. At this point you will still have time to fix any issues that arose from your critique, ultimately creating a stronger final project. This is not to say that the final review is not important. Although you may be finished with the project, or even the studio course, the comments that you get from a final critique will help you learn how to approach the next project in your architectural career.

Another important part of reassessing your project is the final grade that you receive. You may be surprised to find that the results of a critique do not necessarily correlate to a grade. You may have had relatively few negative comments and receive a lower grade that you expected, or better, you may have felt that your critique went poorly, yet are assigned a good grade. Know that despite the comments of the critics, in most cases your grade is ultimately determined by your professor, and may also reflect the amount of work that you do while in studio, or the improvement that you make throughout the semester. While most students become overly stressed about receiving good grades, do not let a poor grade discourage you. Although you may need a higher grade point average for scholarships and graduate school, employers rarely ask for your grades. Instead, focus on constantly improving so that when you graduate you have a portfolio that you can be proud of.

DECIDING

Lori and Chen are standing in the lobby of their school looking at some student projects on the wall and they hear several faculty members talking with a student named Justin. Justin has asked the professors to review his project and give him some critique. Justin's professor is overheard saying, "Justin, we had a crit last Friday where you received many comments, and you have been asking me and other professors for additional comments. We are always happy to give you support and review your work, but be careful: you may become a *crit junkie*." Justin looks a bit confused and his professor continues. "When students are insecure or are very driven to be the best they often get addicted to criticism. This may be because they begin to enjoy the adrenaline of the negative comments, they may feel insecure about their projects, or they may have difficulty making decisions. They are subconsciously shifting responsibility for their project to the professors or critics so that the project is no longer theirs but instead designed by the critics. Think about the future, after you graduate you can no longer call me up for a review of the projects you are working on. You will need to function as a member of a team and make some decisions for yourself."

Deciding is often overwhelming. As students you have all wondered at some point why your professors are not always entirely clear in their criticism. You would like to know specifically what they want from you. You should remember that design involves many small decisions that relate to each other. You might take cues from the other decisions that you have made and, of course, your concept. As was discussed with I. M. Pei's East Wing of the National Gallery in Washington, D.C., the architect envisioned the building as a whole, where the details reflected the conceptual geometry.

Pei allowed the conceptual foundation for the project to inform other decisions in the development process.

You probably have noticed that the projects never feel finished. Deadlines certainly help you finish, but you want to keep working on the project. You are hoping to make it the best possible, but how to know when to finish, and what is finished? During a review of studio projects your instructor may ask that each of you stay to hear all the presentations and criticism. Listening to the critique of your peers hones your skills in criticism. You may speculate what the critics will say, the critics may give comments that apply to everyone's project, and since the projects were the same assignment you can learn from how someone else solved the same issue. This learning will help you with your decision-making process.

It is important to remember that no project will be perfect, as no person is perfect, but you should learn and continue. Part of your education involves the leadership qualities that you will need as you enter the profession. Architects are leaders in that they must enlist a series of others such as clients, contractors, and city officials to unite in the common task of creating a building. However, since buildings have such important abilities to both reflect and persuade society, architects have wider responsibilities than just building a safe structure that adheres to a predetermined budget. As has been said before, architects have traditionally made an important difference concerning how people live. You as a future architect are being educated to make wise decisions. So it is very important that you think about what you are doing in a broad sense. In other words, your decisions have implications and responsibilities.

The experience of assessment and critique can help prepare architects and designers to present a project to clients, officials, and peers in a clear and concise manner, and to receive criticism. Although it may seem stressful at first, the more you, as a student, present your projects, the more skilled you will become in communicating your ideas but also developing a critical eye. By being self-critical, listening to the comments given for different projects, and offering your own opinions, every project will become a learning experience.

When students conclude the design process at the definition stage, they may delude themselves by not addressing the faults of the project. This could ultimately lead to the destruction of the project as its defects come to light during critique. By analyzing the project, it is possible to defend initial ideas, or to return to the previous stage and continue to define the project. The ambiguity of the design process suggests you will always feel off-balance as you need to undergo a long process of iterations. It is important to avoid disillusionment and keep the project fresh. The architectural project is a journey, a journey of discovery and critical thinking. It is misguided to think that the process ends with assessment. Part of the process involves simultaneous thinking. This is not necessarily multitasking but rather understanding the interconnectivity of all aspects of the design. As an analogy, it may be comparable to a dictionary but actually is more akin to a thesaurus. Similar to a rhizome, a vast network of roots, this simultaneous thinking is not sequential but instead multifaceted and complex. Engaging the chaos requires architects and designers to trust in the process and to have faith in the journey. Learning to give over to the investigative journey will prepare you for the next steps in your education and your life in the profession.

Endnotes

1. Two good books on design reviews are, Rosie Parnell, Rachel Sara, Charles Doidge, and Mark Parsons, *The Crit: An Architecture Student's Handbook* (New York: Routledge, 2007) and Kathryn H. Anthony, *Design Juries on Trial* (Champaign: Kathryn Anthony, 2012).

2. See Michel Foucault, "What is Critique," in *The Politics of Truth* (New York: Semiotext(e), 2007).

3. See George Makdisi, "Madrasa and University in the Middle Ages," *Studia Islamica* 32 (1970), 255–264; Hastings Rashdall, *The Universities of Europe in the Middle Ages* (Cambridge: Cambridge University Press, 2010); and Steven Epstein, *Wage Labor and Guilds in Medieval Europe* (Raleigh: University of North Carolina Press, 1995).

4. See Francis Ames-Lewis and Joanne Wright, *Drawing in the Italian Renaissance Workshop* (London: Victoria and Albert Museum, 1983); and Carmen Bambach, *Drawing and Painting in the Italian Renaissance Workshop: Theory and Practice, 1300–1600* (Cambridge: Cambridge University Press, 1999).

5. Anthony, *Design Juries on Trial*, 9. See also Arthur Drexler, ed. *The Architecture of the Ecole des Beaux-Arts* (New York: The Museum of Modern Art, 1977); Donald D. Egbert, *The Beaux-Arts Tradition in French Architecture* (New Jersey: Princeton University Press, 1980); and Robin Middleton, The Beaux-Arts, and Nineteenth-century French Architecture (Cambridge, MA: MIT Press, 1982).

6. Anthony, *Design Juries on Trial*.

7. Ibid.

8. See Frank. H. Bosworth and Roy Childs Jones, *A Study of Architectural Schools* (New York: C. Scribner's Sons, 1932); Mark Jarzombek, *Designing MIT: Bosworth's New Tech* (University of Northeastern Press, 2004); and Walter Gropius, The New *Architecture and the Bauhaus* (New York: The Museum of Modern Art and Faber & Faber, 1936).

9. *The Compact Edition of the Oxford English Dictionary* (Oxford: Oxford University Press, 1971), s.v. "criticism."

10. *Oxford English Dictionary*, s.v. "critical."; *Oxford English Dictionary*, s.v. "criticality."

11. Anthony, *Design Juries on Trial*.

12. Antonio di Piero Averlino, *Treatise on Architecture* (New Haven: Yale University Press, 1965).

13. See Donald Verene, *Hegel's Absolute: An Introduction to Reading the Phenomenology of Spirit* (Albany: State University of New York Press, 2007); and Robert Solomon, *From Hegel to Existentialism* (New York and Oxford: Oxford University Press, 1987).

14. Ibid.

15. See Ernst L. Boyer, *Scholarship Reconsidered: Priorities of the Professoriate: The Carnegie Foundation for the Advancement of Teaching* (New York: John Wiley and Sons, 1990), 15–25.

16. The ACLS Teagle Foundation Working Group on the Teacher–Scholar issued a white paper entitled 'Student Learning and Faculty Research: Connecting Teaching and Scholarship' in May 2007. For more information on the Teacher–Scholar model of education see the American Council of Learned Societies, www.acls.org.

17. Donald Schön, *The Reflective Practitioner: How Professionals Think in Action* (New York: Basic Books, 1984).

18. See G. Vasari, Vasari's *Lives of the Artists: Biographies of the Most Eminent Architects, Painters and Sculptors of Italy*, ed. B. Burroughs (Simon and Schuster, 1945); Moshe Barasch, *Theories of Art, From Plato to Winckelmann* (New York: New York University Press, 1985); Spiro Kostof, *The Architect* (New York: Oxford University Press, 1977); and Marvin Trachtenberg and Isabelle Hyman, *Architecture: From Prehistory to Postmodernism / The Western Tradition* (New Jersey and New York: Prentice-Hall and Harry N. Abrams, 1986).

19. See Albert Speer, *Inside the Third Reich* (New York and Toronto: Macmillan, 1970); and Leon Krier, *Albert Speer: Architecture, 1932–1942* (New York: The Monacelli Press, 2013).

20. Manfredo Tafuri, *The Sphere and the Labyrinth: Avant-Gardes and Architecture from Piranesi to the 1970s* (Cambridge, MA: MIT Press, 1987), 26–37.

Closing

As an architect you design for the present, with an awareness of the past, for a future which is essentially unknown.

Norman Foster

A conclusion is a good place to reflect on what has been discussed, but it is also an opportunity to speculate on the future. A good patron for first year students might be the Roman god, Janus, who represents not only the coming-of-age of young people, but also the duality of past and future. Janus has a double-faced head that allows him to see both in front and behind, suggesting the relationship between memory and speculation, things we have done and things we will do.

C.1 Head of Janus, Vatican museum

Janus is also important for architects, since he resides on the thresholds between past and present, old and new, and inside and outside. While a threshold can be simply a transition from one space to another, a threshold can also symbolize enlightenment, and the movement between stages in our lives. Thresholds not only allow the flow of air, but also suggest the possibility for ideas to pass between past and future. Janus is also concerned with transition and ambiguity, since a threshold is not entirely inside or entirely outside, and may be considered as neutral or non-committed. Thresholds play a part in beginnings and are symbolic in traditions such as marriage where crossing a threshold celebrates a couple's new life together. Janus therefore represents the potentialities and possibilities of the future.

This conclusion will speculate on how an ending can also be a beginning. To begin, it is important to summarize some of the main points of *Developing your Design Process: Six Key Concepts for Studio* as a foundation for a discussion of some key issues that will influence your future as an architect. It is hoped that if you can look back at what you have just learned about design, it will help you look forward to more clearly engage the future of architectural education and professional practice.

LOOKING BACK / THE PREVIOUS CHAPTERS

The design studio is a unique environment in that it requires much more than just the development of technical skill. From the initial assignment description to the final critique, studio courses use conceptual language to encourage you to think critically about the projects, something few students will have previously considered or been prepared for. It does not matter if you are just starting out or already well-established in the design field, understanding the design process can be challenging.

The chapters have attempted to explain basic ideas about critical thinking to help you in your own design process. It is hoped that these chapters have offered students of architecture a way to begin to understand the reasons behind steps in the design process, ultimately enabling better decisions and stronger design concepts.

The previous chapters have attempted to explain the importance of understanding the design process, allowing you to delve deeper into your projects and think with more clarity. While not a definitive recipe for design, this book has established six important concepts of any design process and explained why keeping each in mind can help architects and designers create more thoughtful projects.

The first concept is about beginnings. It concerned creating something that you desire and attempted to identify the characteristics of an architect as well as the importance of educating oneself in design culture. In order for any architecture student to be successful, they must ensure that they are doing something that they ultimately desire. There also must be some sense of discipline to architectural work, so that passion and imagination are balanced with skills and knowledge.

The second concept is about the process of imagining. It concerns developing an architectural concept and explored the spark of imagination that leads to a strong thematic direction. Bringing a new idea into existence is often a combination of speculation and guessing. Developing a method of discourse is also a crucial step in the design process for its ability to imagine different scenarios and ideas before the actual analysis takes place.

The third concept deals with playing. This section discussed the notion of spending time with your idea. Once a concept has been hatched, one needs to quickly deliberate and yet still spend time with it. There is a certain amount of delay that is acceptable, and even required before moving on to a full analysis of the concept. The adage *festina lente*, to hurry slowly, represents a dichotomy that students must keep in mind during this stage.

The fourth concept concerns choosing. Once a sufficient amount of time has been spent with an idea, it must be decanted to ensure that only the clear, useful parts are retained. This stage deals with separating an idea into its parts and deleting the inappropriate, all while distilling and focusing the appropriate. This is the point where decisions are edited down to what is essential to get closer to a goal.

Concept five involves defining. It explored focusing the original concept and making an abstract idea visible. It is essential that once an idea is decided upon it be defined and described in any form possible. This could include drawings, models, or other forms of description that begin to detail the idea and bring it to life. This not only determines the boundaries of the idea and checks to see that all the essential information is there, but it also delivers it into the public realm for others to see and understand.

The final and sixth concept investigates assessing. It encouraged stepping away for a moment and critically questioning the concept by identifying strengths and weaknesses. When students conclude the design process at the definition stage, they delude themselves by not addressing the faults of the project. This could ultimately lead to the termination of the project as its flaws come to light during critique. By deconstructing the project, it is possible to defend initial ideas, or to return to the previous stage and continue to define the project.

While the above chapters represent a general idea of the progression from inspiration to critique, they should not be thought of as a means to an end. The design process is iterative, and a certain amount of flexibility and ambiguity is to be embraced. This process is often challenging for students and requires the progression through a number of stages to fully understand and develop a concept. The initial inspiration or conception is perhaps the most elusive, and the idea of divine design is a common starting point. Divining is about portending the future and is a process of reading signs and symbols to determine an outcome, and, subsequently, it is the architect's responsibility to interpret the signs of the site or the project requirements to make appropriate decisions. Initially the possibilities for a design are endless, but after inspiration, these potentialities begin to diminish as the concept is defined.

While this book has been developed to assist future architects, it should not be seen to exclude designers because they must be well versed in all aspects of design. Likewise, architects should understand basic principles that generate design. This is also why you will find architects designing chairs, interiors, graphics, industrial designs as well as buildings. When you design you are creating, fashioning, executing, and constructing a physical manifestation of an idea. It is through this creative process of design that your intentions are defined. The entirety of design consists of a broad foundation of thinking of which architecture is but a part. Most fields of design believe the novice should start with design basics. You should not think just in terms of formulistic principles, nor solely in your chosen discipline, but of how to think like a designer.

LOOKING FORWARD / THOUGHTS ABOUT YOUR FUTURE

Thinking as a designer is the first step but, in most cases, you will need further education in your chosen discipline. As an early year design student interested in becoming an architect, you may be enrolled in a bachelor program, a graduate program – one where you have a non-related undergraduate degree, or entering a first professional degree doctoral program.[1] In each of these instances, you are looking forward to more complex projects as you progress through your education. You, most likely, have been observing the studios of upper year students or have attended the design reviews of more advanced students. This is a very good habit. It may be advantageous to introduce yourself to these students since they may act as mentors. Hearing them discuss their projects can help you learn by trying to understand their conceptual thinking. In the computer lab, they can certainly clarify some difficult applications and help you navigate certain processes. The more experienced students can be invaluable resources when choosing elective courses and managing the bureaucracy of your academic program of study. Seeing and hearing other more accomplished students can provide perspective on the progress of your education.

Thinking about the immediate future is important if you are required to attend graduate school in order to be a licensed architect. Typically, architecture schools evaluate graduate applications considering undergraduate grades, scores on the Graduate Record Exam, your letter of intent, letters of recommendation, and a portfolio.

Grading practices for design studio can be confusing to first year students. Sometimes more quantifiable issues such as craft, attendance, and effort may be weighted heavily, but this is not always the case. When grading your work, one professor may find certain issues more important than another professor. These could be issues such as how much you explored, investigated, researched, synthesized, and applied the concepts, principles, and methods of the assignment in your project. However, other issues may also be considered, for example if you miss a series of studios, are endlessly late to class, turn in late projects, or are always missing required supplies, it

C.2 Visitors to General Motors'
"Futurama"exhibit

will probably affect your grade. It is true that your studio
instructors will interpret your designs based on their
own belief system. Nevertheless, first year instructors
are typically hired because they are experienced design
teachers, open minded, and generally fair in their analysis
of your work. Some schools use the first year to cull out
the weak students and thus, grading can be competitive.
Other schools limit the number of students in early years
by using high admission standards and consequently, first
year grading is less strenuous, possibly even pass/fail.
Grades are seen as a measure of your development and a
demonstration of acquired skills in creativity and applied
judgment. Whatever the system used by a design school
for grading individual or group creative work, it is rarely
precise. While design schools know that grades can be
imprecise they do remain important to the university or

college as a whole. Scholarships, grants, and awards can all be determined by your grade point average. Universities may require graduate architecture programs to impose a grade point average such as a "B" or above when accepting students. Although some potential employers may look at your grade point average they usually do not. They are much more interested in another determination of your skills, your portfolio of design work.

Today, most architecture offices require a portfolio for employment and professional academic programs for admission. Preparation of a portfolio involves documenting the best projects from your undergraduate studios and thus should be started well before you graduate. A portfolio is a set of images either bound in book form or loose in a folder. In the case of architecture, a portfolio shows a collection of the best of an individual's work relevant to the field, and demonstrates design growth, talent, and interests. According to the Association of Collegiate Schools of Architecture, "Most schools of architecture will require a portfolio review as part of the admissions process, whether you are applying directly from high school, from within an undergraduate program, or as a returning graduate student. In all these instances, the strongest portfolios tend to be those that demonstrate the creative potential of the candidate, and emphasize the unique strengths and talents that the prospective student can bring to the school's program."[2]

A typical example of a portfolio requirement is from Harvard University / Graduate School of Design stating that applicants must submit a portfolio that includes their most important and representative design work. The portfolio for Master in Design Studies and Doctor of Design applicants may include research or academic papers as well as a design component, if relevant to the applicant's area of study. Yale School of Architecture requires a portfolio, not to exceed nine by twelve inches and no more than one and one-half inches thick, containing reproductions (no slides, tapes, discs, or videos will be accepted) of creative work done by the applicant, showing drawing skills and three-dimensional aptitude. Work represented may include drawings, paintings, sculpture, sketches, furniture, and architectural designs, or other materials.

Portfolios are generally judged in comparison to criteria such as how they demonstrate an overall understanding of design ability, direction of work, clarity of position, and general quality and craft. They evaluate students' ability to demonstrate complex architectural ideas visually. Faculty members look for students' ability to not only integrate complex mechanical systems and building codes into the design of buildings, but also contemporary thoughts about how humans should reside. Faculty members interpret the work and assess the potential abilities of applicants. They judge the work subjectively, by looking at students' ability to clearly define the concept of a specific piece of architecture by integrating such ideas into the objective of the building itself. Faculty members can also assess less subjective outcomes in the work that involve presentation and graphic ability. The best and quickest way professors are able to judge students' potential design ability is through evaluating a portfolio.

When it is time to apply for a position in an architectural office, you will also need a portfolio. Most jurisdictions, especially in North America, require internship for architecture registration and licensure. In the United States, after you graduate from an accredited school of architecture you will need to work three years for an architect to become licensed. The architectural design internship offers a graduated student the opportunity to gain experience. Such programs as the Intern Development Program allow graduates to assist a senior architect and log hours in the areas of planning, development, and production, for example. Internship is a bridge between school and the responsibilities of the profession. Interns work under the direction of a licensed architect and are given various tasks to help them learn, first hand, the many aspects of design in the delivery of an architectural project. The architectural design internship exposes you to decision-making processes, project management, construction management, and the work culture of architects and engineers. The field of architecture is very complex, and the internship serves as an extension of your education as an architect. After a number of years of experience, and the accomplishment of specific learning outcomes, interns will be allowed to sit for the professional examination.[3]

Although the economic downturn in North America has limited architectural commissions over the last few years, this trend is not expected to continue. The U.S. Bureau of Labor Statistics projects the employment outlook for architects is expected to grow 24% between 2010 and 2020. The growth in Canada is expected to exceed the U.S. numbers. This growth is faster than average for all occupations.[4] These statistics indicate a greater need for architects, especially those with knowledge of sustainable design. Although the trend is promising, there will still be competition for jobs. The most competition will be for positions in prestigious architectural firms, and students who have distinguished themselves in design will have an advantage. Prospective employers will be looking at your degree and the school where you attended but they will also be looking for other qualifications. They will try to assess your personal skills such as responsibility, honesty, and work ethic. They will try to comprehend your communication, technical, and organizational skills through an interview. When viewing your portfolio they will be looking for your creative, visualization, and critical thinking abilities. Many of these skills you have learned in school, but they will also consider traits that you have developed over a lifetime.

Because design school prepares students in the broad areas of creativity and critical thinking, besides the technical skills necessary for the profession, students may find career satisfaction in other creative fields. If you graduate with an undergraduate degree such as a BA/BS in environmental design there are many options for you. Some of you will continue with graduate education in architecture, but other potential areas of study may include urban and regional planning, industrial design, animation, interior design, landscape architecture, construction management, or graphical design to name a few. You may also use your background to specialize within areas of the discipline such as lighting design, building material research and manufacture, acoustics, building safety, or energy efficiency consulting. Design and architecture educated graduates also have skills in creative and critical thinking that would be valuable in fields such as law, medicine, engineering, or business/entrepreneurial activities. The ability to look at issues in an analytical, critical, or holistic manner would prove useful for various jobs.

LEARNING / THE FUTURE OF ARCHITECTURAL EDUCATION

Architectural education in North America, with its foundations in the École des Beaux Arts and the Bauhaus, has evolved over the years. Although the emphasis of each school is different, they all have the same goal – to educate students for the profession of architecture. Since most state and provincial registration boards require any applicant for licensure to have graduated from an accredited program, obtaining such a degree is essential for becoming a professional architect.

The National Architecture Accreditation Board (NAAB) in the United States and Canadian Architecture Certification Board (CACB) in Canada accredit schools of architecture that offer professional degrees.[5] Accredited status acknowledges that a program meets at least minimal standards for its faculty, curriculum, student services, and libraries, and that the program rises to standards needed to educate an architect. Accreditation is a form of quality assurance as these boards govern a foundation of criteria that need to be satisfied, but still allow each school to structure their own curriculum and pedagogical approach. Accreditation stipulates, in the conditions and procedures for accreditation, periodic campus visits and satisfaction of student performance criteria. Student Performance Criteria evaluate evidence of student projects, papers, and exams to see if they satisfy specific criteria in areas such as design integration, graphic communication, history and theory, technical skills, and professional practice. Every few years, the bodies review the terms of accreditation, and as a result make changes. Any changes to the processes and criteria are made in collaboration with collateral organizations, such as the state or provincial registration boards, the national school councils and student organizations. Architectural education is always in flux considering such things as changing technologies, new information and ideas, and pedagogical research. Decisions to alter the terms of accreditation always reflect changes or trends in the profession. The flexibility of the accreditation process encourages individual schools' initiatives such as experiential learning opportunities for design/build or international exchanges.

PRACTICING / THE FUTURE OF THE PROFESSION

Unable to predict the future with complete certainty, it is nevertheless possible to analyze current trends to anticipate what the future will hold. The profession of architecture has seen substantial change and will encounter more in the next decades. Certainly the construction materials and processes to deliver architectural projects are changing. New processes for design and project management have grown out of integrated project delivery, as there is greater need to communicate and collaborate with all participants. Research into, and development of, new building materials and composites have increased buildings' energy efficiency. Architects have been reconsidering the basic materials we use to build, especially in light of green building guidelines and concern for a sustainable future. Advances in digital technology have and will continue to change all aspects of architecture, from design processes to construction and facilities management. Digital technology will continue to assist communication, analysis, and construction.

Architectural societies have over the last several years recognized the importance of altruist endeavors to better the lives of people around the world.[6] They are questioning how architecture, and architects, can assist developing countries and in the instances of natural disasters. Architects have the skills and talents to be of assistance in many areas of the environment and should take their responsibilities seriously. Architects' engagement in the world community is vital to the recognition of the importance of architecture by society. Many architects are now and will in the future question how the discipline can retain its relevancy. Part of being continually relevant is engagement in current discussions about the future and how people live. Architects must be committed to a program of life-long learning.

Firms like Bjarke Ingels Group (BIG) have established a new means of communication with the community in illustrating their design philosophy. They were savvy enough to use the emergence of the new Internet design blogs, like Arch Daily and Dezeen, to make themselves known in the architectural world. Recognizing the Internet's need for content, they entered every competition available and cranked out models and images of architectural forms on the landscape. With actual architecture magazines and journals giving way to the ease and editorial freedom of the Internet, BIG began to profit immensely within this new age of social media.

SHIFTING / THINGS THAT CHANGE AND THINGS THAT STAY THE SAME

When we talk about continuing education, particularly in the United States and Canada, you probably think of non-degree career training, workforce training, formal personal enrichment courses (both on-campus and online), and self-directed learning (such as through Internet interest groups). Architectural licensing bodies can impose continuing education requirements on their members who hold licenses. These requirements may be satisfied through college or university coursework, extension courses, conferences and seminar attendance, and in a variety of other ways. Usually such requirements are imposed to keep architects technically current. There is, however, another good reason to continue to be educated in an array of subjects. If you consider architecture as directly influencing the way people live in the world through our buildings, then larger questions need to be considered. These are questions such as why we are here, how we should live and what our relationship is to nature. These questions are not easily answered, and have been the basis of inquiry since the first humans on earth viewed the stars. This search can be exciting and it can easily keep you interested throughout your life. The more you learn of the world, the better you can engage these questions. Activities such as reading on various topics, traveling, developing new skills, and experiencing different things can all be helpful in your search for answers. Of course, designing buildings is also part of this search as each new structure offers a possible way to answer difficult questions. Ask yourself, if I as an architect do not take responsibility in this, who will?

There is a famous quote that states, "The more things change, the more they remain the same."[7] We refer to this quote because it offers an important way to consider change within the field of architecture. The basic argument, as it applies to architecture, is that no matter how many technical advances are made in the field, human nature and society remain pretty much the same. It is important to take a quick look at the two issues involved. Today, most architecture firms rely on the use of computers in the design process. Computer Aided Design drawings can be worked on in the office during the day and sent overseas to be further developed during the night. Again, new materials offer architects' offices expanded design possibilities, and digital fabrication allows new freedom in creating new and unusual forms. Many of these changes were almost inconceivable thirty years ago. Yet for all these changes the people who inhabit these spaces remain remarkably similar to humans from thousands of years ago. People in the past and present, love and fear the unknown, hope for security and safety for their families, and need protection from the elements. In other words, no matter how much technical progress is made, human society is similar to what it was when culture emerged. A study of history reveals an example of this. Looking to evidence of ancient graffiti that makes rude comments or scrawls things such as "Aufidius was here," or "Marcus loves Spendusa" helps us to understand how people were very much the same then as they are today.[8]

If the past can inform the future, then we need to return to the discussion of Janus. His unique position of looking backward and forward should be the position of architects, since they should learn from the past, and anticipate and prepare for the future. As stated by Abraham Lincoln "The best way to predict your future is to create it!" This lesson should be heeded if we are to influence the future of architecture and society.

Endnotes

1   "National Architectural Accrediting Board (NAAB)," www.naab.org; "Canadian Architectural Certification Board (CACB)," www.cacb.ca

2   See Association of Collegiate Schools of Architecture (ACSA) Guide to Schools.

3   For internship, licensure, and registration see American Institute of Architects (AIA), National Council of Architectural Registration Boards (NCARB), Canadian Architectural Certification Board (CACB), Canadian Architectural Licensing Authorities (CALA).

4   "US Bureau of Labor Statistics Outlook for Architects," www.bls.gov/ooh/Architecture-and-Engineering.htm.

5   For more on accreditation, see National Architectural Accrediting Board (NAAB) and Canadian Architectural Certification Board (CACB).

6   See "Union Internationale des Architectes (UIA)," uia-archtectes.org; and "Royal Architectural Institute of Canada (RAIC)," raic.org.

7   The quote is attributable to Jean-Baptiste Alphonse Karr (1908–1990). Karr's actual words were: 'plus ça change, plus c'est la même chose' (Les Guêpes). However, I believe that Karr's words have been quoted by several other luminaries, from George Bernard Shaw to Winston Churchill.

8   "Ancient Roman Graffiti," www.pompeiana.org.

Index